Rotary Roundup

Rotary Roundup

40 More Fast & Fabulous Quilts

JUDY HOPKINS & NANCY J. MARTIN

That Patchwork Place®

MISSION STATEMENT

WE ARE DEDICATED TO PROVIDING QUALITY PRODUCTS THAT ENCOURAGE CREATIVITY AND PROMOTE SELF-ESTEEM IN OUR CUSTOMERS AND OUR EMPLOYEES.

WE STRIVE TO MAKE A DIFFERENCE IN THE LIVES WE TOUCH.

That Patchwork Place is an employee-owned, financially secure company.

Rotary Roundup ©
© 1994 by Judy Hopkins and Nancy J. Martin

That Patchwork Place, Inc.,
PO Box 118, Bothell, WA 98041-0118
USA

Printed in Hong Kong
99 98 97 96 95 94   6 5 4 3

Library of Congress Cataloging-in-Publication Data

Hopkins, Judy,
   Rotary Roundup / Judy Hopkins and Nancy J. Martin.
      p.   cm.
   ISBN 1–56477–028–1:
      l. Patchwork—Patterns. 2. Cutting. 3. Quilting—
   Patterns.
I. Martin, Nancy J. II. Title.
TT835.H574 1994   93-27838
746.9'7—dc20   CIP

Acknowledgments

Special thanks are extended to:

Ella Bosse, Jackie Carley, Debby Coates, Elinor Czarnecki, Lavonne DeBoer, Rosie Huntemann, Sarah Kaufman, Julie Kimberlin, Dee Morrow, Cleo Nollette, Louise Pease, Terri Shinn, Jeanie Smith, Mariet Soethout, George Taylor, and Bridget Walsh, for providing quilts;

Roxanne Carter, Marta Estes, Donna K. Gundlach, Peggy Hinchey, Julie Kimberlin, Beatrice Miller, Hazel Montague, Alvina Nelson, Beverly Payne, Nancy Sweeney, and Sue von Jentzen, for their fine quilting;

Cleo Nollette, for her generous help in cutting, stitching, illustrating, and pattern testing.

Credits

Editor-in-Chief . . . . Barbara Weiland
Technical Editor . . . . Susan I. Jones
Managing Editor . . . . Greg Sharp
Copy Editor . . . . Liz McGehee
Text and Cover Design . . . . Judy Petry
Typesetting . . . . Laura Jensen
Photography . . . . Brent Kane
Illustration and Graphics . . . . Laurel Strand
                                              Karin LaFramboise

Contents

Introduction

When you love to make quilts as much as we do, the thrill of starting another quilt is always beckoning. We both enjoy making multi-fabric quilts from the fabric stashed on our shelves or stored in scrap bags. To indulge in this passion, we rotary cut and speed piece, allowing us the time to make even more quilts.

The overwhelming popularity of our previous book, *Rotary Riot,* affirmed to us that many of you share our compulsive quiltmaking and fabric-buying traits. We received thank-you notes for providing rotary-cutting directions and new fabric combinations for the traditional blocks that we all dearly love. In addition, we received an overwhelming number of requests for another book providing the same type of quilts and information.

We both brainstormed, trying to come up with ways to improve this second book. In the end, we decided, "If it isn't broken, don't fix it"—except for a few minor variations we couldn't resist.

All the basics on rotary cutting are presented in the front of the book. If you are not familiar with these techniques, then be sure to read this section. If you are accomplished at rotary cutting, then just check Judy's new information on trimming templates, and Nancy's use of fat quarters for making bias squares. Using fat quarters as the unit of measurement when cutting bias strips for bias squares has many advantages: there is virtually no waste, and you can make use of more fabrics in creating multi-fabric quilts.

Both of us are definitely in a multi-fabric or scrap-quilt mode at present. Judy is working directly from her scrap bag, using her ingenious tool, the ScrapSaver™, to recycle her fabrics. Nancy continues to "round up" many variations of fabrics within a color family as she makes her quilts. Wonderful fabrics purchased while on teaching trips in Australia, Holland, and Belgium have made their way into many of the quilts in this new book of rotary-cut quilts.

We hope you like the quilts that are part of our "roundup" and that you enjoy many happy hours making them.

Nancy and Judy

Gallery

Pastel quilts create a light, casual air in this informal sitting room. *Cleo's Castles in the Air* is hung on the wall; *Walkabout* is folded across the back of the chair.

In this inviting living room, a *Fine Feathered Star* quilt hangs above the sofa and a *MilkyWay* quilt is folded over the back of the love seat.

Chinese Puzzle provides the perfect accent on the back wall of this blue-and-white kitchen.

One great quilt, like this *Amsterdam
Star,* can create an exciting entryway.

A *Four Corners* quilt
complements the beige
striped sofa, while a
folded *Puss-in-the-Corner*
quilt provides an accent.

A *Pot of Flowers* quilt is casually draped over the bed in contrast to *Bridal Path,* which is carefully folded to hang from the door of the armoire.

An antique *Double Irish Chain* quilt covers the bed and complements the clear, clean lines found in this small bedroom.

A child's bedroom is enhanced by the *Tin Man* and *Hearts and Hourglass* quilts.

Materials and Supplies

Rotary Cutter and Mat

A large rotary cutter enables you to quickly cut strips and pieces without templates. A self-healing mat with a rough finish holds the fabric in place and protects both the blade and table on which you are cutting. An 18" x 24" mat allows you to cut long bias strips. A smaller mat is ideal when working with scraps.

Cutting Guides

You need a ruler for measuring and to guide the rotary cutter. There are many appropriate rulers on the market, but a favorite is the Rotary Rule™. It is made from ⅛"-thick Plexiglas and includes markings for 45° and 60° angles, guidelines for cutting strips, plus the standard measurements. The Rotary Mate™ is a 12"-long cutting guide with the same features. The Bias Square® is the tool most critical to bias strip piecing. This acrylic cutting guide is available in three sizes, 4", 6", and 8" square, and is ruled with ⅛" markings. It features a diagonal line, which is placed on the bias seam, enabling you to cut two accurately sewn half-square triangles. The Bias Square is convenient to use when cutting small quilt pieces, such as squares, rectangles, and triangles. The larger 8" size is ideal for quick-cutting blocks that require large squares and triangles as well as making diagonal cuts for quarter-square triangles. A 20cm-square metric version is also available for those who prefer to work in this format.

The ScrapSaver™ cutting guide is a tool designed for cutting individual half-square triangles in a variety of sizes from scraps.

All of the cutting guides are available from That Patchwork Place, Inc., P.O. Box 118, Bothell, WA 98041-0118.

Sewing Machine

You need a straight-stitch machine in good working order. Make sure the tension is adjusted so that you are producing smooth, even seams. A seam that is puckered causes the fabric to curve, distorting the size of your piecing. Use a new needle in the machine to avoid snags and thread pulls in the fabric. (Old needles usually make a popping sound as they enter the fabric.)

Needles

Use sewing-machine needles sized for cotton fabrics (size 70/10 or 80/12). You will also need hand-sewing needles (Sharps) and hand-quilting needles (Betweens #8, #9, #10).

Pins

You should have a good supply of glass- or plastic-headed pins. Long pins are especially helpful when pinning thick layers together.

Iron and Ironing Board

Frequent and careful pressing are necessary to ensure a smooth, accurately stitched quilt top. Keep your iron, ironing board, and a plastic spray bottle of water close to your sewing machine.

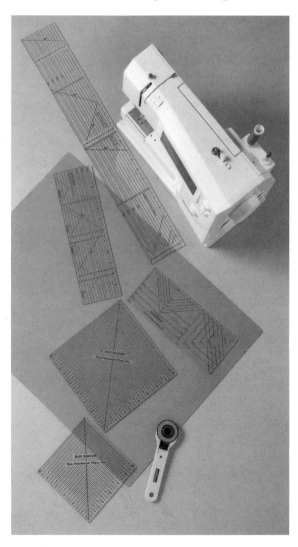

Fabric

FABRIC SELECTION

For best results, select lightweight, closely woven, 100% cotton fabrics. Polyester content may make small patchwork pieces difficult to cut and sew accurately.

While 100% cotton is ideal, it is not always possible with quilts created from fabric collections of long-standing. We purchased some of our most interesting prints before we followed the 100% rule—they are polyester/cotton blends of uncertain content. While it is best not to use these, the colors and prints are unobtainable today and often serve a unique design purpose in a quilt.

FABRIC LIBRARY

Many of the quilts in this book are multi-fabric quilts, commonly referred to as "scrap quilts." The success of a multi-fabric quilt, which relies on color groups rather than the use of a single print in a certain color, is dependent upon a well-stocked "fabric library" or scrap bag. Making multi-fabric quilts can change your fabric shopping.

Nancy rarely purchases specific fabric for a specific quilt. When she buys new fabric, it is with the goal of enriching her fabric library. She buys three to four yards of any fabric that would make a good background fabric. These are mainly lighter fabrics—white, beige, taupe, ecru, pink, lavender, and blue with a white background. She buys from one-half to two yards of medium- to dark-toned prints, depending on how much she likes the color and design.

FAT QUARTERS

Many of the yardage amounts specify fat quarters. This is an 18" x 22" piece of fabric (rather than the standard quarter yard that is cut selvage to selvage and measures 9" x 44"). The fat quarter is a more convenient size to use, especially when cutting bias strips for bias squares. For added convenience, most quilt shops offer fat quarters already cut and bundled. Look for a basket or bin of fat quarters when buying fabrics.

If you are having trouble choosing a color scheme, you might want to select a bundle of fat quarters that has been color-coordinated. Often, you can use this group of fabrics as the basis for an effective color scheme, purchasing additional background fabric and more of any fabric that you wish to feature in your quilt.

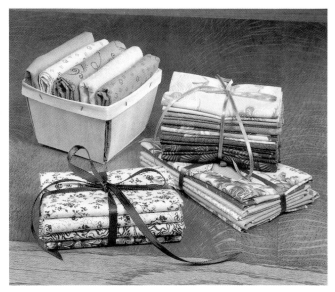

COLOR RECIPE

Working with a color recipe will add variety to your quilt. Select a quilt or block and study its design. Assign a color family to a particular area of the block. An example is shown below.

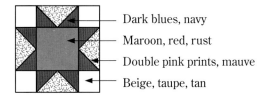

— Dark blues, navy
— Maroon, red, rust
— Double pink prints, mauve
— Beige, taupe, tan

Next, select a run of colors for each color family, pulling a variety of prints and visual textures from your fabric library. Do not overmatch the colors chosen, but select a range of colors. For instance, if you make a color run of red fabrics, select maroons, deep reds, rusty reds, true reds, and possibly even a warm brown print with red overtones. As you stitch each block, combine different fabrics from the various color families, adhering to your fabric recipe. Try to make blocks with high contrast and ones with low contrast. The result will be a multi-fabric quilt, where each block is not identical but is unified by the repetition of colors in the color recipe.

It's fun to make a quilt following a fabric recipe because each resulting block will be different. Feel free to experiment with unusual prints and color arrangements. Push yourself; be adventurous. Go beyond what you consider "safe" fabric and color usage. Break a few rules. Forget about centering large motifs. Cabbage roses and other large prints work better when they are cut randomly—even off grain if you wish. Try using the wrong side of some prints to get just the right tone. If you make a mistake in piecing, consider leaving it in to create interest. Most of all, have fun as you try the many options that will make your quilt unique.

If you are working entirely from fabrics on hand, your fabric and color choices will depend on what is available in your scrap bag or fabric library. Some quilt patterns call for an assortment of light and dark fabrics, others for a combination of lights, mediums, and darks. In the pattern section of this book, a shaded block outline may show only one or two "fabrics" for a particular value range. When you are working with scraps or collected fabrics, you may be using a number of different fabrics to represent a single value. When cutting the pieces shown as "dark" in the shaded outline, for example, you could use two, three, or ten different dark fabrics. These might be all the same color (such as an assortment of dark blues) or different colors of the same value (such as a combination of dark blues, dark greens, and dark browns).

It is difficult and not really desirable to maintain consistency in value and contrast in a scrap-bag quilt. Your "light" fabrics may range from light to medium, your "dark" fabrics from medium to dark. Contrast may vary from block to block; the pattern may stand out more in some areas of the quilt than in others. Remember, much of the charm of the scrap quilt lies in its variety. Simply do the best you can with what you have and enjoy the inconsistencies and contradictions that will invariably result.

SAMPLE BLOCKS

Once you have determined your color recipe and pulled color runs of fabric from your fabric library, it is time to test the recipe by making sample blocks. Study the sample block illustration found with each quilt to cut the pieces needed for one sample block.

In a multi-fabric quilt, it is necessary to make several sample blocks to determine the effectiveness of the color recipe. Overuse of a color, color integration, contrast, and unity are hard to determine in a single block.

FABRIC PREPARATION

Wash all fabrics first to preshrink, test for colorfastness, and get rid of excess dye. Continue to wash fabric until the rinse water is completely clear. Add a square of white fabric to each washing of the fabric. When this white fabric remains its original color, the fabric is colorfast. A cupful of vinegar in the rinse water may also be used to help set difficult dyes.

Make it a habit to wash and prepare fabrics after you buy them and before you place them in your fabric library. Then, your fabric will be ready to sew when you are.

Rotary Cutting

GRAIN LINES

Yarns are woven together to form fabric, giving it the ability to stretch or remain stable, depending on the grain line you are using. Lengthwise grain runs parallel to the selvage and has very little stretch. Crosswise grain runs from selvage to selvage and has some "give" to it. All other grains are considered bias. True bias is a grain line that runs at a 45° angle to the lengthwise and crosswise grains.

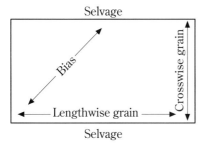

If fabric is badly off grain, pull diagonally as shown to straighten. It is impossible to rotary cut fabrics exactly on the straight grain of fabric since many fabrics are printed off grain. In rotary cutting, make straight, even cuts as close to the grain as possible. A slight variation from the grain will not alter your project.

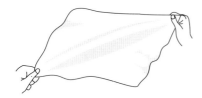

In most cases, you will find that rotary-cutting directions use the following guidelines for grain-line placement:

1. Strips are cut on the crosswise grain of fabric.
2. Squares and rectangles are cut on the lengthwise and crosswise grain of fabric.
3. Half-square triangles are cut with the short sides on the straight grain and the long side on the bias. Bias strip piecing produces sewn half-square triangles that have grain lines that follow this guideline.
4. Quarter-square triangles have the short sides

on the bias and the long side on the straight grain. They are generally used along the outside edges of individual blocks or quilts where the long edge will not stretch.
5. When you are working with striped fabric or directional prints, the direction of the stripe or print takes precedence over the direction of the grain. Handle these pieces carefully since they might not be cut on grain and will therefore be less stable. If you are going to use these pieces along the outside edges of the quilt, staystitch ⅛" from the raw edges to prevent stretching.

STRAIGHT CUTS

Cut all pieces with the ¼"-wide seam allowance included. If you sew accurate ¼" seams by machine, there is no need to mark stitching lines. To cut squares, rectangles, and triangles, you will first need to cut straight strips of fabric.

1. Align the Bias Square with the fold of fabric and place a cutting guide to the left. When making all cuts, place fabric to your right. (Reverse these techniques if you are left-handed.)

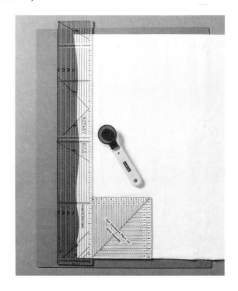

2. Remove the Bias Square and make a rotary cut along the right side of the ruler. Hold the ruler down with your left hand, placing the little

finger off the ruler to serve as an anchor and to keep the ruler from moving. Move your hand along the ruler as you make the cut, making sure the ruler remains in place. Use firm, even pressure as you rotary cut. Begin rolling the cutter before crossing onto the folded fabric edge and continue across the fabric. Always roll the cutter away from you; never pull the cutter toward you.

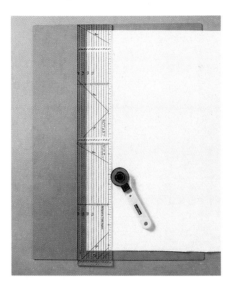

3. Fold fabric lengthwise again so that you will be cutting four layers at a time. (This means shorter cuts.) Open and check the fabric periodically to make sure you are making straight cuts. If fabric strips are not straight, use the Bias Square, cutting guide, and rotary cutter to straighten the edge again.
4. Place all fabric to the right and measure from the left straight edge. You can combine the Bias Square with other rulers to make cuts wider than 3½".

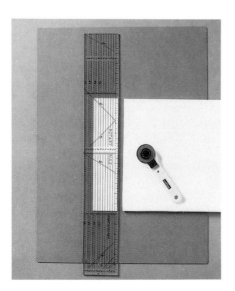

BIAS CUTS

Cut bias strips for bias squares and binding in the following manner:

1. Align the 45° marking on the ruler along the selvage and make a bias cut.
2. Measure the width of the strip from cut edge of fabric. Cut along edge of ruler.

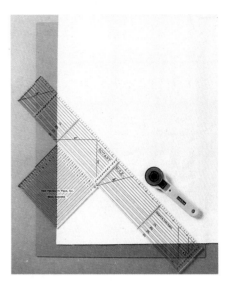

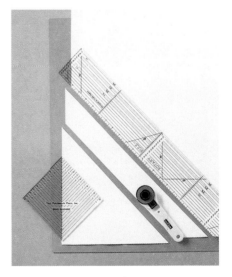

SQUARES AND RECTANGLES

1. First cut fabric into strips the measurement of the square, including seam allowances.
2. Using the Bias Square, align the top and bottom edge of the strip and cut fabric into squares the width of the strip.
3. Cut rectangles in the same manner, first cutting the strips to the shortest measurement of the rectangle.

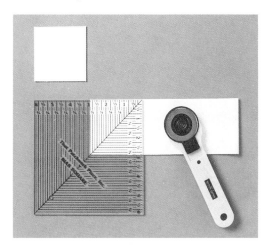

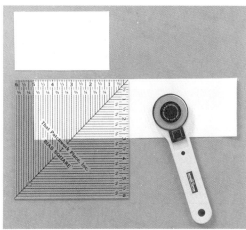

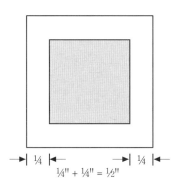

4. To cut a small, odd-sized square or rectangle for which there is no marking on your cutting guide, make an accurate paper template (including ¼''-wide seam allowances). Tape it to the underside of the Bias Square and you will have the correct alignment for cutting strips or squares.

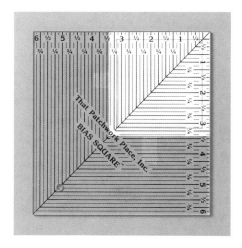

HALF-SQUARE TRIANGLES

Most of the triangles used in these quilts are half-square triangles. These triangles are half of a square, with the short sides on the straight grain of fabric and the long side on the bias. To cut these triangles, cut a square and then cut it in half diagonally. Cut the square ⅞'' larger than the finished short side of the triangle to allow for seam allowances.

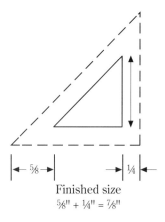

Finished size
⅝'' + ¼'' = ⅞''

1. Cut a strip the desired finished measurement, plus ⅞''.
2. Cut strip into squares, using the same measurement.

3. Cut a stack of squares diagonally, from corner to corner.

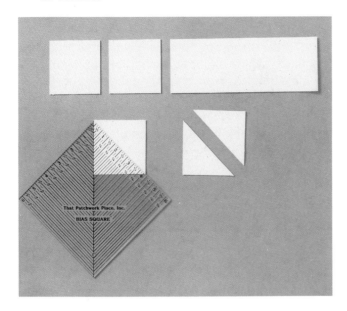

Trimming Points for Easy Matching

You can use the Bias Square to trim seam-allowance points on half-square triangles. The measurement to use is the finished short side of the triangle, plus ½" (¼"-wide seam allowance on each side). The example shown here is a half-square triangle with a finished dimension of 4".

1. To quick-cut this triangle, cut a 4⅞" square of fabric and cut it in half diagonally.
2. To trim the points for easy matching, set the Bias Square at the 4½" mark on the fabric triangle as shown. The points of the triangle will extend ⅜"; trim them off with the rotary cutter.

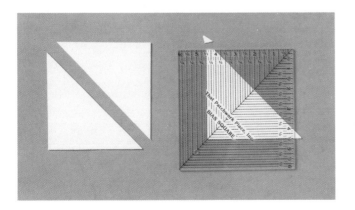

QUARTER-SQUARE TRIANGLES

Triangles with the longest sides along the outside edges of blocks and quilts are usually quarter-square triangles. These triangles are cut from squares so their short sides are on the bias and the long side is on the straight of grain, making them easier to handle and keeping the outside edges of your quilt from stretching. Cut the square 1¼" larger than the finished long side of the triangle.

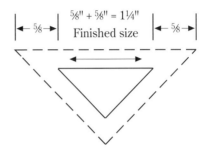

1. Cut a strip the desired finished measurement, plus 1¼".
2. Cut the strip into squares.
3. Cut the squares in half diagonally, lining up the ruler from corner to opposite corner. Without moving these pieces, cut in the other direction to create the **X** cut. Each square will yield four triangles with the long side on grain.

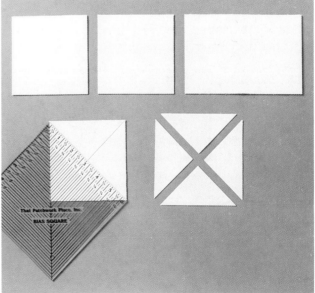

TRIMMING TEMPLATES

Some quilt designs include squares or rectangles that have one or more corners trimmed off at a 45° angle, allowing you to add a triangle from a different fabric. The traditional Snowball block is a typical example.

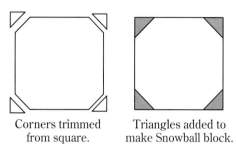

Corners trimmed   Triangles added to
from square.   make Snowball block.

In this book, a "trimming template" outline is provided with patterns that require these shapes. Carefully trace the outline onto stiff, clear plastic and cut out the shape. The outline is the correct size as given: *Never add seam allowances to a trimming template!*

Cut the needed squares or rectangles as described in the basic cutting instructions. Stack these in layers of four and place the trimming template in one corner, aligning the two short sides of the trimming template with the outside edges of the squares or rectangles. Hold the trimming template down firmly and push your Bias Square against the long edge of the template; the plastic will stop the ruler at the proper position. Move the trimming template out of the way and cut along the ruler to remove the corner. Repeat for other corners if instructed to do so.

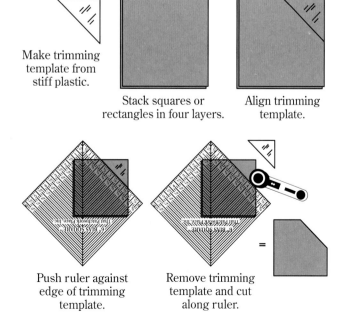

Make trimming
template from
stiff plastic.

Stack squares or   Align trimming
rectangles in four layers.   template.

Push ruler against   Remove trimming
edge of trimming   template and cut
template.   along ruler.

An alternate method is to lay your Bias Square upside down over the appropriate trimming-template outline, aligning the long side of the trimming template with the outside edge of the Bias Square. Then, outline the two short sides of the trimming template with masking tape on the underside of the Bias Square. You can also make a cutout from lightweight plastic or cardboard and tape it to the underside of the Bias Square. Align the edges of the masking tape or the cutout with the corner of your stack of squares or rectangles; remove the corner by cutting along the edge of the Bias Square.

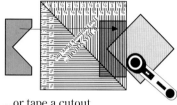

Outline the   ...or tape a cutout   ...then trim.
trimming template   to the underside
with masking tape...   of a ruler...

PAPER TEMPLATES

It is sometimes necessary to use a paper template while rotary cutting, especially if the template is a difficult shape or is cut in $\frac{1}{16}$" or $\frac{1}{8}$" increments. Using the templates found in this book, trace the desired shape, including seam allowances, onto paper. Cut template from paper, and tape to the underside of the rotary ruler, aligning the straight edge with the edge of the ruler. Use the paper template, rather than the ruler markings, to cut the desired shape.

BIAS SQUARES

Many traditional quilt patterns contain squares made from two contrasting half-square triangles. The short sides of the triangles are on the straight grain of fabric while the long sides are on the bias. These are called bias-square units. Using a bias strip-piecing method, you can easily sew and cut bias squares in many sizes. This technique is especially useful for small bias squares, where pressing after stitching usually distorts the shape (and sometimes burns fingers).

Basic Technique

1. To make fabric more manageable, cut two fat quarters (18" x 22") of contrasting fabric and layer with right sides facing up. You will cut both fabric strips at the same time.

2. Use the 45° marking on the cutting guide and a longer ruler to make a bias cut. The cutting chart on page 24 will tell you how far from the lower left corner to make your first bias cut.

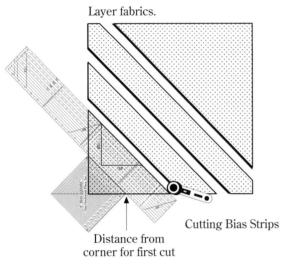

Layer fabrics.

Cutting Bias Strips

Distance from corner for first cut

3. In most cases, cut strips the same width as the size of bias squares you need. For example, cut bias strips 2½" wide for 2½" unfinished bias squares. After piecing, you will have 2" finished bias squares. This general rule is easy to remember, but specific strip widths are provided with the quilt directions.

4. Sew the strips together on the long bias edge with ¼"-wide seams, offsetting the tops of the strips ¼" before stitching the seam as shown. Press the seams toward the darker fabric. (If cutting bias squares 1¼" or smaller, you may want to press the seams open to evenly distribute the fabric bulk.

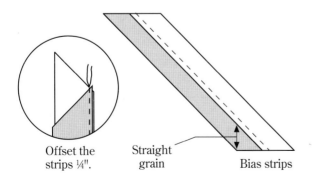

Offset the strips ¼".

Straight grain

Bias strips

5. Align the 45° marking of the Bias Square with the seam line. Cut the first two sides. Turn the strip. Align the 45° mark with the seam line, and the cut edges with the desired measurement of the unfinished bias square; cut the third and fourth sides.

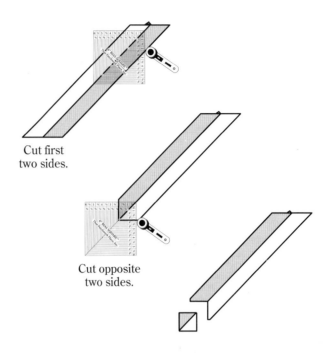

Cut first two sides.

Cut opposite two sides.

6. Align 45° marking on the Bias Square with the seam line before cutting the next bias square.

Note: All directions in this book give cut size for bias squares; finished size after stitching will be ½" smaller.

MULTIPLE BIAS SQUARES

To conserve time and fabric, use the following method to mass produce bias squares. Cut all strips from fat quarters, 18" x 22" pieces of fabric. The directions specify the fabrics to use and the width of the strips to cut.

1. Layer two fat quarters of fabric with right sides facing up and cut as shown above. The cutting chart on page 24 lists the distance from the lower left corner for the first cut.

2. Join all the strips along the long bias edge, using ¼"-wide seams and alternating colors. Remember to offset strips as shown at left. From each set of fat quarters, you will have two units of two fabrics pieced together.

The units will vary in size and shape, depending on the placement of the first cut and the width of the strips. Here is what the units for the most common sizes will look like:

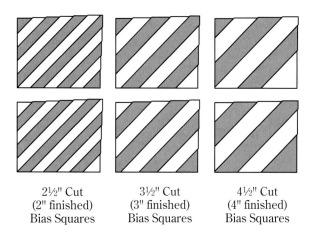

2½" Cut
(2" finished)
Bias Squares

3½" Cut
(3" finished)
Bias Squares

4½" Cut
(4" finished)
Bias Squares

3. Begin cutting at the left side on the lower edge of each unit. Align the 45° marking of the Bias Square on the seam line and cut the first two sides slightly larger than the desired cutting size. Continue across the row.

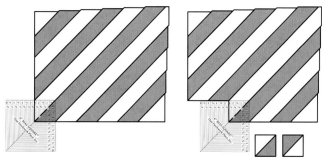

Align 45° marking on seam line and cut first two sides.

Continue across the row.

Note: For scrappier quilts, increase the number of bias-square fabric combinations by cutting strips from 3 or more fat quarters and combining the strips at random into multi-fabric units.

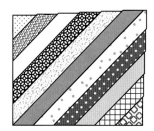

4. Turn the cut segments and place the Bias Square on the opposite two sides, accurately aligning the measurements on both sides of the cutting guide and the 45° marking. Cut the remaining two sides of the bias squares according to the exact cutting measurement.

Turn cut segments and cut opposite two sides.

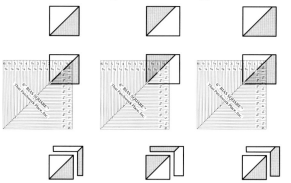

5. Continue cutting bias squares in this manner, working up the strip-pieced unit, row by row, until you have cut bias squares from all usable fabric. The chart below specifies how many bias squares you can expect to cut from two fat quarters of fabric.

Fat Quarters Cutting Chart for Bias Squares
*Based on 1 light and 1 dark fat quarter,
18" x 22", of fabric*

First* Cut	Strip Width	Cut Size	Finished Size	Yield
2½"	1¾"**	1½"	1"	176
3"	2"**	1¾	1¼"	126
3"	2"	2"	1½"	112
3"	2¼"	2¼"	1¾"	84
4"	2½"	2½"	2"	60
4"	2¾"	3"	2½"	50
4½"	3"	3½"	3"	40
5"	3¾"	4½"	4"	21

*First cut is the distance from the left corner.
**Press seams open rather than toward dark fabric.

SQUARE TWO AND OTHER RELATED UNITS

While working on the bias square concept as introduced in *Back to Square One,* Marsha McCloskey and Nancy J. Martin discovered that they could construct other units by cutting the bias squares in half. Marsha introduced these units in her book *On to Square Two.* All of the units begin with the basic bias square, cut the size specified in the directions.

Square Two

1. Stack two bias squares right sides together, with opposing color placement and seam allowances.

2. Draw a diagonal line from corner to corner. Stitch ¼" away from the drawn line on both sides.

Stitching lines

3. Cut diagonally along the drawn line.

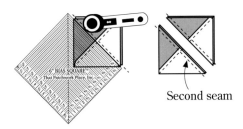
Second seam

4. Press the seam to one side and trim the ends. You will have two Square Two units.

Unit 1.5

1. Cut a bias square in half diagonally.

2. Join each unit to a triangle of the same size. You will have a Unit 1.5 and a reverse Unit 1.5.

Unit .5

1. Cut a bias square in half diagonally.

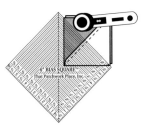

2. You will have a Square .5 and a reverse Square .5.

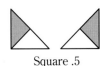
Square .5

MULTI-FABRIC QUILTS FROM SCRAPS

Using the ScrapSaver™ cutting guide, you can quickly cut half-square triangles in an assortment of useful sizes from your odd-shaped scraps.

To quick-cut half-square triangles, we typically add ⅞" to the desired finished size of a short side of the triangle, cut a square to that measurement and divide the square on the diagonal. This technique allows for ¼"-wide seam allowances and yields two half-square triangles, with the short sides on the straight grain of the fabric and the long side on the bias.

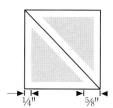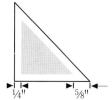

Finished size of short side
of triangle plus ⅞" = cut size

With the ScrapSaver tool, you can quick-cut individual half-square triangles without first cutting a square. The tool is marked for cutting 1⅞", 2⅜", 2⅞", 3⅜", and 3⅞" half-square triangles; with ¼"-wide seams, the short sides will finish to 1", 1½", 2", 2½", and 3".

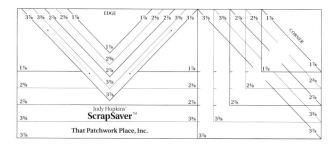

To use the ScrapSaver, you will need a rotary cutter and a cutting mat. A small cutting mat is ideal because you can rotate the mat to get the proper cutting angle without disturbing the fabric. Press your scraps before you begin, then cut as described in the following paragraphs. You can stack several scraps for cutting. Place the largest piece on the bottom and the smallest piece on top, aligning any square corners or true bias edges.

Remember the following guidelines:
For 1" (finished) triangles, use the 1⅞" lines.
For 1½" (finished) triangles, use the 2⅜" lines.

For 2" (finished) triangles, use the 2⅞" lines.
For 2½" (finished) triangles, use the 3⅜" lines.
For 3" (finished) triangles, use the 3⅞" lines.

For scraps with square corners (common with bias-square edge triangles):
Align the corner of the scrap with the proper edge-triangle lines of the ScrapSaver and cut along the straight edge to remove excess fabric.

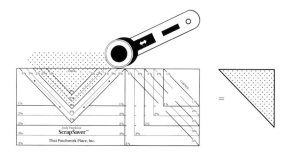

For scraps with true bias edges:
Align the bias edge of the scrap with the proper corner-triangle line of the ScrapSaver and cut along the two straight edges to remove excess fabric.

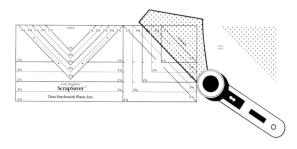

For scraps with no square corners or true bias edges:
Lay the corner triangle of the ScrapSaver over the scrap, aligning the ruler with the grain of the fabric and making sure that the corner-triangle line for the size you wish to cut does not extend beyond the fabric. Cut along the two straight edges, making a square corner.

Note: It may be easier to find the grain by looking at the wrong side of the fabric.

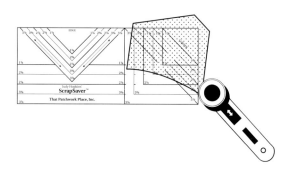

Align the square corner with the proper edge-triangle lines and cut along the straight edge to remove the excess fabric.

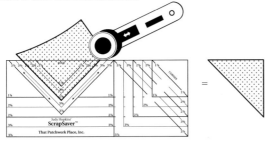

For larger scraps:

Lay the corner square of the ScrapSaver over the scrap, aligning the ruler with the grain of the fabric and making sure that the corner-square lines for the size you want to cut do not extend beyond the fabric. Cut along the two straight edges, making a square corner.

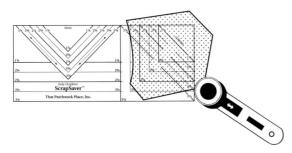

Rotate the cutting mat or turn the cut piece of fabric, align the corner you just cut with the proper corner-square lines, and cut along the two straight edges again to make a square.

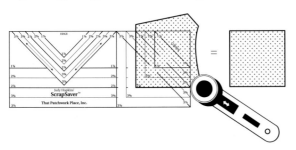

Align a corner of the square with the proper edge-triangle lines and cut along the straight edge to divide the square into two triangles.

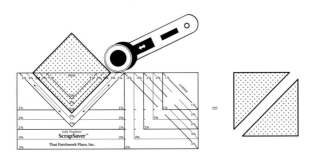

For large rectangular scraps:

Align a long edge of the ScrapSaver with the grain of the fabric and cut along the ruler to remove the uneven edge of the scrap.

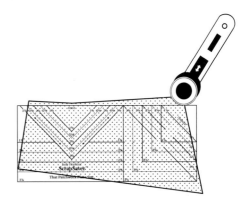

Rotate the cutting mat or turn the cut piece of fabric and align the proper long line with the straight cut you just made; cut along the two straight edges to make a square corner.

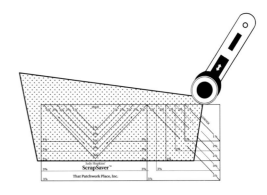

Align a square corner with the proper corner-square lines and cut along the straight edge to complete the square.

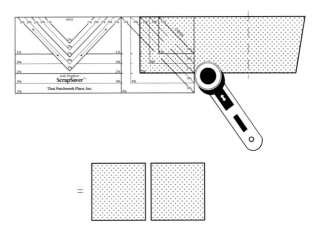

Repeat until you have cut as many squares as possible from the strip. Divide the squares, using the proper edge-triangle lines as shown above.

Machine Piecing

A well-maintained, straight-stitch sewing machine is adequate for all quiltmaking operations. Use sewing machine needles sized for cotton fabrics (size 70/10 or 80/12) and change them frequently; dull or bent needles can snag and distort your fabric and cause skipped stitches. Set stitch length at 10–12 stitches per inch; make sure the top and bobbin tensions are properly adjusted. Judy uses a medium greenish-gray thread for piecing all but the lightest and darkest fabrics—the color you get when you mix all the Easter egg dyes together. If an even-feed ("walking") foot is available for your machine, it is worth buying one. You will find it invaluable for sewing on bindings and for machine quilting.

Learn to sew a precise ¼"-wide seam. Find the ¼"-wide seam allowance on your machine by placing an accurate template under the presser foot and lowering the needle onto the seam line; mark the seam allowance by placing a piece of masking tape or moleskin at the edge of the template.

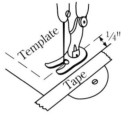

You can save time and thread by chain piecing. Place the pieces you are joining right sides together; pin as necessary. Stitch the seam, but do not lift the presser foot or cut the threads; just feed in the next set of pieces as close as possible to the last set. Sew as many seams as you can; then clip the threads between the pieces.

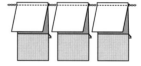

Appliqué

Some of the quilts in this book have appliquéd accents. Use the paper-patch appliqué technique that follows. When stems are required as in "Pot of Flowers" on page 87, use the bias strip method described below.

PAPER-PATCH APPLIQUÉ

1. Make a stiffened template of each shape in the appliqué design. Do not add seam allowances to the templates.
2. On bond-weight paper or freezer paper, trace around the stiffened templates to make a paper patch for each shape in the appliqué.
3. Pin each paper patch to the wrong side of the fabric. If using freezer paper, pin with plastic-coated side facing out.

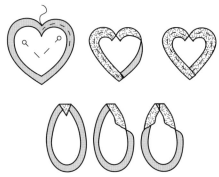

4. Cut out fabric shapes, adding a ¼"-wide seam allowance around each paper shape.
5. With your fingers, turn the seam allowance

over the edge of the paper and press or baste to the paper. If you baste, do inside curves first. (A little clipping may be necessary to help the fabric stretch.) On outside curves, take small running stitches through the fabric only, to ease in fullness.

Paper   Paper

Take an occasional stitch through the paper to hold fabric in place. Follow this basting order (inside curves first, outside curves last) when appliquéing the fabric piece to the block, easing fullness and bias stretch outward.

BIAS STRIPS

One of the most satisfying techniques for creating smooth stems uses metal or heat-resistant plastic bias bars. Bias or Celtic bars are sold in quilt shops. Hobby and craft stores sell similar bars in a variety of sizes.

1. Cut bias strips the length and width specified in the pattern.

2. Fold bias strip in half, wrong sides together, and press.
3. Stitch ⅛" from raw edges, creating a tube.

4. Insert the bias bar into the tube and twist the tube to bring the seam to the center of one of the flat sides of the bar.

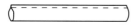

5. Press the seam flat with an iron.

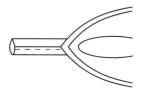

6. Remove the bar. The raw edge is now pressed out of sight on the underside of the tubing, and there are two evenly folded edges to appliqué. Pin the bias strips into position.

STITCHING

When all the seam allowances are turned and basted, press the appliqué pieces. Then position and pin the pieces in place on the background fabric. Template numbers identify each appliqué piece and indicate the order in which you should sew them. Be sure to appliqué each piece in the correct sequence, or you will find yourself taking out stitches to tuck in other pieces.

1. Use a small, blind-hemming stitch and a single strand of matching thread (i.e., green thread for a green leaf) to appliqué shapes to the background fabric.
2. Start the first stitch from the back of the block. Bring the needle up through the background fabric and through the folded edge of the appliqué piece.

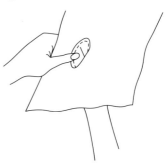

3. Insert the needle right next to where you brought it up, but this time put it through only the background fabric.
4. Bring the needle up through the background fabric and into the appliqué piece, approximately ⅛" or less from the first stitch.
5. Space your stitches a little less than ⅛" apart.
6. When appliqué is complete, slit the background fabric and pull out the paper patch.

Quilt Patterns

This section contains complete instructions for forty rotary-cut quilts. All of the patterns are written for rotary cutting; no templates are provided except for quilts with appliqué or trimming templates. Read the complete cutting and piecing directions for the quilt you are going to make before you begin. The patterns are graded with symbols as to difficulty, so match the pattern to your skill level.

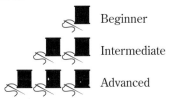

Beginner

Intermediate

Advanced

The "Materials" section of each pattern includes fabric and color suggestions. Fabric requirements are based on 44"-wide fabric that has 42 usable inches. If, after preshrinking, your fabric is not at least 42" wide, you may need to purchase more.

Cutting dimensions are given for strips that are 42" long when cut across the fabric width. If your preshrunk fabric is wider than 42", it is not necessary to cut away the excess. If it is narrower than 40", you might need an additional strip of fabric to cut the required number of pieces.

Most of the quilts using bias squares call for the purchase of fat quarters. Measure the fat quarters to ensure they are 18" x 22". Smaller fat quarters may require the purchase of additional fabric. Always cut the largest pieces first from the fat quarters, before cutting the smaller pieces.

To achieve a scrappy look, we purchased a variety of fat quarters. You may not always use all of the fat quarter of fabric, so save it for your next scrappy quilt.

Cutting instructions are geared for rotary cutting. Quick-cutting and strip-piecing techniques sometimes yield more pieces than are needed to make a particular block or quilt; don't worry if you have a few more pieces than you need. All measurements include ¼"-wide seam allowances. *Do not add seam allowances to the dimensions given in the cutting section.*

Cutting specifications for triangles indicate the size of the square from which you will cut the triangles. Directions for half-square triangles instruct you to "cut once diagonally"; for quarter-square triangles, they tell you to "cut twice diagonally." If you need a refresher, see the section that begins on page 20.

Half-Square Triangles
Cut once diagonally.

Quarter-Square Triangles
Cut twice diagonally.

Quick-cutting methods vary from pattern to pattern; in each case, we have selected the technique most appropriate to the particular quilt. For example, some patterns that include half-square triangle units use the Bias Square technique; others might instruct you to cut ScrapSaver triangles or standard quick-cut triangles and join them into half-square triangle units. All of the methods used are thoroughly explained in the section on rotary cutting (pages 18–27).

Use the photos and drawings that accompany the patterns as a reference while assembling your quilt. If you need help setting blocks on point, see the section that begins on page 120.

Most quilts have borders with straight-cut corners rather than mitered corners, except where otherwise noted. You can cut border strips along the crosswise grain and seam where extra length is needed; purchase additional fabric if you want to cut borders along the lengthwise grain. Cut border pieces extra long, then trim to fit when you know the actual dimensions of the center section of the quilt. (See "Borders" section, beginning on page 124.)

Bindings are narrow, double-fold, and made from straight-grain or bias strips. (See the "Binding" section, beginning on page 129, if you need basic information on applying bindings.)

In several of the patterns, the instructions result in a quilt that differs in dimension from the quilt in the photograph.

General instructions for finishing your quilt begin on page 119.

Amish Ninepatch Scrap

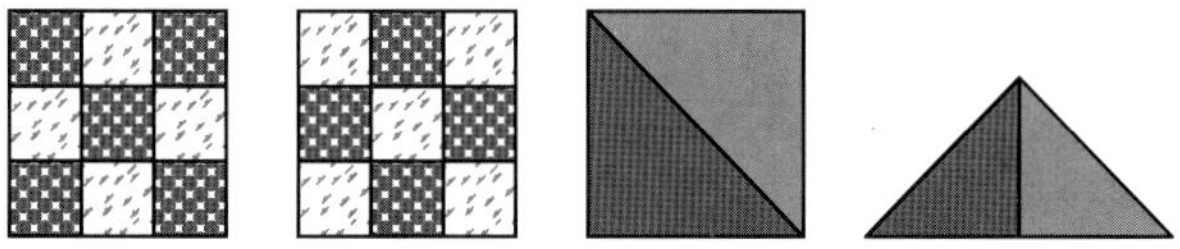

Block A
4½" block

Block B
4½" block

Block C
4½" block

Half Block D

Dimensions: 57" x 89"

116 blocks (33 Block A, 33 Block B, 50 Block C, and 10 Half Block D), 4½", set on point 6 across and 11 down; 1½"-wide inner border with corner squares and 8"-wide outer border with corner squares.

Note: The pictured quilt has pieced corner squares in the inner border; the pattern calls for plain corner squares.

Materials: 44"-wide fabric

⅛ yd. each of 11 different light prints for Blocks A and B

⅛ yd. each of 11 different medium and/or dark prints for Blocks A and B

¼ yd. each of 10 different medium and/or dark solids for Block C, Half-Block D, and side setting triangles

4½" x 9" medium or dark solid for corner setting triangles (Nearest cut is ⅛ yd.)

⅜ yd. bright pink solid for inner border

2" x 8" red solid for inner border corners (Nearest cut is ⅛ yd.)

2⅛ yds. blue-green solid for outer border

¼ yd. purple solid for outer border corners

5⅜ yds. fabric for backing

⅝ yd. fabric for 310" of narrow binding

Batting and thread to finish

Cutting: All measurements include ¼" seams.

From each of the 11 light and 11 medium and/or dark prints:

Cut 3 strips, 2" x 20", for a total of 33 light and 33 medium and/or dark strips for Blocks A and B.

From each of the 10 medium and/or dark solids:

Cut one square, 7⅝" x 7⅝", for a total of 10 squares. Cut twice diagonally into 40 quarter-square triangles for side setting triangles. You will have 20 triangles left over; save them for another project.

Cut 5 squares, 5⅜" x 5⅜", for a total of 50 squares. Cut once diagonally into 100 half-square triangles for Block C.

Cut 1 square, 4⅛" x 4⅛", for a total of 10 squares. Cut once diagonally into 20 half-square triangles for Half Block D.

From the 4½" x 9" solid:

Cut 2 squares, 4⅛" x 4⅛". Cut once diagonally into 4 half-square triangles for corner setting triangles.

From the bright pink solid:

Cut 6 strips, 2" x 42", for inner border.

From the 2" x 8" red solid scrap:

Cut 4 squares, 2" x 2", for inner border corners.

From the blue-green solid:

Cut 4 strips, 8½" wide by the length of the fabric (2⅛ yds.) for outer border.

From the purple solid:

Cut 4 squares, 8½" x 8½", for outer border corners.

DIRECTIONS

1. Select 3 of the light print strips (all the same fabric) and 3 of the medium and/or dark print strips (all the same fabric) and join to make 2 strip units as shown. The units should measure 4½" wide when sewn. Cut each unit into 9 segments, each 2" wide.

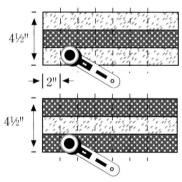

2. Join the segments to make 3 Block A and 3 Block B.
3. Repeat steps 1 and 2 with the remainder of the light print strips and the medium and/or dark print strips, for a total of 33 Block A and 33 Block B.
4. Join the 5⅜" assorted solid half-square triangles to make 50 Block C. Combine the

fabrics at random.

5. Join the 4⅛" assorted solid half-square triangles to make 10 Half Block D. Combine the fabrics at random.

6. Set the blocks together in diagonal rows with the side and corner triangles. (See "Assembling On-Point Quilts" on page 122.) Join the rows as shown in the quilt photo. Trim and square up the outside edges after the rows are sewn, if needed.

7. Add pink inner border, seaming strips as necessary and adding red corner squares. Follow the directions for "Borders with Corner Squares" on page 125.

8. Add blue-green outer border and purple corner squares, as for inner border.

9. Layer with batting and backing; quilt or tie. See page 133 for a quilting suggestion.

10. Bind with straight-grain or bias strips of fabric.

Ninepatch Exchange *by George Taylor, 1993, Anchorage, Alaska, 57" x 89".*
George combined Ninepatch blocks acquired in a block swap with scraps
of rich Amish solids to make this lively quilt. Quilted by Peggy Hinchey in an
original wavy-line pattern that has become George's trademark.

Amsterdam Star

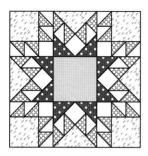

Amsterdam Star
16⅞" block

Dimensions: 77⅝" x 77⅝"

9 blocks, 16⅞", set 3 across and 3 down with 3¼"-wide sashing and sashing squares; 7"-wide border.

Materials: 44"-wide fabric

9 fat quarters of assorted beige prints for star
   backgrounds
10 fat quarters of assorted green prints for star
   "feathers" and sashing squares
5 fat quarters of assorted red prints for star tips
1½ yds. red print for sashing
2⅜ yds. striped fabric for border and star centers
   (must have at least 4 repeats across the width)
4½ yds. fabric for backing
⅝ yd. fabric for 314" of narrow binding
Batting and thread to finish

Cutting: All measurements include ¼" seams.

From each fat quarter of beige print:
   Cut 4 squares, 2½" x 2½", for Unit I.
   Cut 4 squares, 2⅜" x 2⅜", for Unit II.
   Cut 1 square, 6⅞" x 6⅞". Cut twice diagonally
into 4 triangles (36 total) for Unit I.
   Cut 4 squares, 4¼" x 4¼", for Unit II.

From each fat quarter of green print:
   Cut 4 squares, 2⅞" x 2⅞". Cut once diagonally
into 8 triangles (80 total) for Unit I.

Pair the remainder of the assorted fat quarters of green and beige prints:
   Cut and piece 2½"-wide bias strips, following the directions for making bias squares on page 23. From this pieced fabric, cut 8 bias squares, 2½" x 2½", and 16 bias squares, 2⅜" x 2⅜".

Note: Be careful to keep these bias squares in two separate sets. The larger bias squares are used in Unit I, and the smaller bias squares are used in Unit II.

From the remaining fat quarters of green print:
   Cut 16 squares, 3¾" x 3¾", for sashing squares.

From each fat quarter of red print:
   Cut 8 squares, 3¾" x 3¾". Cut once diagonally into 16 triangles (80 total) for Unit I.

Note: You will need 8 matching triangles for each star. There will be 8 triangles left over.

From the red print for sashing:
   Cut 24 pieces, 3¾" x 17⅜", for sashing strips.

From the striped fabric for border:
   Cut 4 strips, 7¼" x 81", for striped border.
   Cut 9 squares, 6⅛" x 6⅛", for star center.

DIRECTIONS

1. Piece 36 of Unit I, using the 2½" x 2½" bias squares in beige and green; 2½" x 2½" beige squares; large beige and red triangles; and small green triangles.

Note: You will need 8 matching red triangles for each star.

Unit I
Make 36.

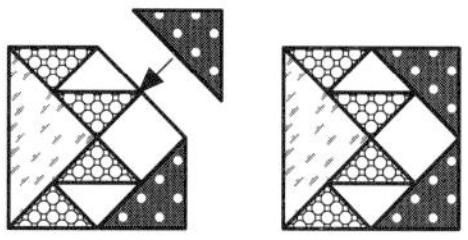

2. Piece 36 of Unit II, using the 2⅜" x 2⅜" bias squares in green and beige; 2⅜" x 2⅜" beige squares; and the 4¼" x 4¼" beige squares.

Unit II
Make 36.

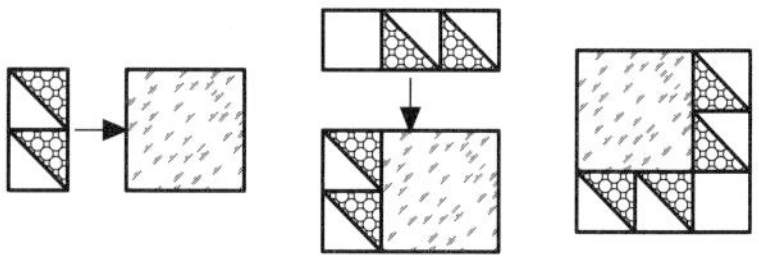

3. Piece 9 Amsterdam Star blocks, using 1 center square of striped border fabric, 4 Unit I, and 4 Unit II squares for each block.

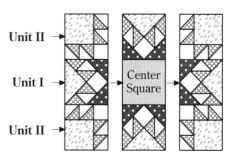

Unit II →

Unit I → Center Square →

Unit II →

4. Join blocks into rows, using 3 blocks and 4 sashing pieces.
5. Assemble 4 rows of sashing, using 3 sashing strips and 4 sashing squares.
6. Assemble rows of blocks with rows of sashing between them as shown in the quilt photo.

7. Add striped border, seaming strips as necessary. See "Borders with Mitered Corners" on page 125.
8. Layer with batting and backing; quilt or tie. See page 133 for a quilting suggestion.
9. Bind with straight-grain or bias strips of fabric.

Amsterdam Star *by Nancy J. Martin, 1992, Woodinville, Washington, 77½" x 77½".*
A wonderful reproduction striped chintz or "sitz" fabric purchased from den haan
and wagenmakers *in Amsterdam, Netherlands, serves as the center of each Feathered
Star and creates a graceful swirling border. Exquisitely quilted by Alvina Nelson.*

Art Square

Art Square
8" block

Sawtooth Star
8" block

Dimensions: 76" x 92"

80 blocks (40 Art Square and 40 Sawtooth Star), 8", set 8 across and 10 down; 6"-wide border.

Materials: 44"-wide fabric

8 fat quarters of assorted, large-scale prints or chintzes with light background for Art Square centers

10 fat quarters of assorted red plaids and checks for Art Square blocks

4 fat quarters of dark blue large-scale prints or chintzes for Sawtooth Star centers

10 fat quarters of assorted blue plaids, checks, and stripes for Sawtooth Star blocks

1½ yds. navy blue print for border

5½ yds. fabric for backing

⅝ yd. fabric for 346" of narrow binding

Batting and thread to finish

Cutting: All measurements include ¼" seams.

From each fat quarter of large-scale print or chintz with light background:
Cut 5 squares, 6⅛" x 6⅛", for Art Square centers.

From each fat quarter of red plaids and checks:
Cut 16 squares, 2½" x 2½", for Art Square corners.
Cut 16 squares, 2⅞" x 2⅞". Cut once diagonally into 32 triangles (320 total) for Art Square blocks.

From each fat quarter of dark blue large-scale print or chintz:
Cut 10 squares, 4½" x 4½", for Sawtooth Star centers.

From each fat quarter of blue plaid, check, or stripe:
Cut 16 squares, 2⅞" x 2⅞", from the lighter fabrics. Cut once diagonally into 32 triangles (320 total) for Sawtooth Star tips.
Cut 4 squares, 5¼" x 5¼". Cut twice diagonally into 16 triangles (160 total) for Sawtooth Star blocks.

Cut 16 squares, 2½" x 2½", for Sawtooth Star corners.

From the navy blue print for border:
Cut 8 strips, 6¼" x 42".

DIRECTIONS

1. Piece 40 Art Square blocks, using the red fabrics. Use a different combination of red plaid and checked fabric as you make each block, but keep the triangle fabric and corner square fabric the same within each block.

Make 4.

2. Piece 40 Sawtooth Star blocks, using the blue fabrics. Use different combinations of blue plaid, checked, and striped fabric as you make each block, keeping the star tips, corner squares, and large triangles the same within each block.

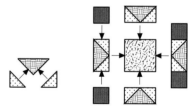

3. Join together in rows of 8 blocks, alternating the Art Square and Sawtooth Star blocks. Join rows together as shown in the quilt photo

4. Add navy blue border, seaming strips as necessary. See "Borders with Straight-Cut Corners" on page 124.
5. Layer with batting and backing; quilt or tie. See page 133 for a quilting suggestion.
6. Bind with straight-grain or bias strips of fabric.

Art Square *by Mariet Soethout, 1990, Amsterdam, Netherlands, 76" x 92". Lively plaid, check, and chintz fabrics, collected from fabrics used for costumes in various Dutch villages, lend an air of excitement to this two-block quilt. Mariet based her design on* A Dozen Variables *by Nancy J. Martin and Marsha McCloskey, published by That Patchwork Place, Inc., 1988. (Photo courtesy of* den haan *and* wagenmakers.*)*

Baskets of Chintz

Baskets of Chintz
10" block

Dimensions: 96" x 96"

36 blocks, 10", set on point with plain alternate blocks, corner and side setting triangles; 5½"-wide border with pieced corner blocks.

Materials: 44"-wide fabric

9 fat quarters of assorted dark red and blue plaids, checks, and stripes

5 yds. muslin for bias squares, alternate blocks, and setting triangles

5 fat quarters of assorted chintz fabrics for basket centers

9 fat quarters of assorted light red and blue plaids, checks, and stripes

1½ yds. light chintz print for border

8½ yds. fabric for backing

¾ yd. fabric for 392" of narrow binding

Batting and thread to finish

Cutting: All measurements include ¼" seams. Templates on page 40.

From each fat quarter of the dark red and blue plaids, checks, and stripes:

Cut 2 squares, 6⅞" x 6⅞". Cut once diagonally into 4 triangles (36 total) for basket base.

Cut 4 squares, 2⅞" x 2⅞". Cut once diagonally into 8 triangles (72 total) for basket base.

From muslin:

Cut 9 pieces, 12" x 18". Pair each with the remainder of the fat quarters of assorted dark red and blue plaids, checks, and stripes.

Cut and piece 2½"-wide bias strips, following the directions for making bias squares on page 23. From this pieced fabric, cut 252 bias squares,

2½" x 2½". You will need 7 matching bias squares for each basket.

From the remainder of the muslin:

Cut 25 squares, 10½" x 10½", for the alternate blocks.

Cut 5 squares, 15½" x 15½". Cut twice diagonally to make 20 side setting pieces.

Cut 2 squares, 8" x 8". Cut once diagonally to make 4 corner setting pieces.

Cut 2 strips, 1¾" x 42", for the half-length diamonds. Using Template A, cut 16 diamonds for the corner squares. (See page 22 for directions on using paper templates.)

From each fat quarter of chintz fabric for basket centers:

Cut 4 squares, 6⅞" x 6⅞". Cut once diagonally into 8 triangles (40 total) for basket centers. You will have 4 triangles left over.

From 1 chintz fat quarter:

Cut 4 squares, 2⅝" x 2⅝", for center of pieced corner blocks (Template C, page 40).

From each fat quarter of light red and blue plaids, checks, and stripes:

Cut 8 rectangles, 2½" x 6½".

Cut 2 squares, 4⅞" x 4⅞". Cut once diagonally into 4 triangles (36 total).

Cut 2 half-width diamonds using Template B. You will use 16 for the corner squares. (See page 22 for directions on using paper templates.)

From the light chintz print for border:

Cut 8 strips, 6" x 42".

DIRECTIONS

1. Piece 36 Basket blocks as shown. Vary the coloration on about one-third of the blocks, placing the dark side of the bias squares as shown in the inset photo on page 39.

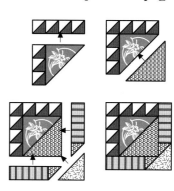

Baskets of Chintz *(with detail) by Mariet Soethout, 1989, Amsterdam, Netherlands, 96" x 96". Chintz or "sitz" fabric was used for the center of each charming basket. Plaids and checks of various sizes and scale form the baskets, which are surrounded by a reproduction chintz border with pieced corner squares. (Photo by Rob Sas, Fotostudio, Arnhem, The Netherlands.*

2. Join Basket blocks into diagonal rows with alternate blocks and side and corner setting pieces.

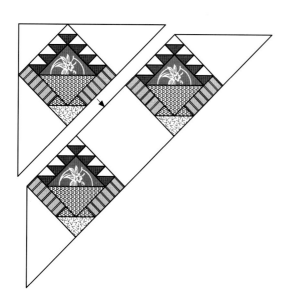

3. Join rows together to form quilt top.

4. Piece the 4 corner squares, using pieces cut from Templates A, B, and C.

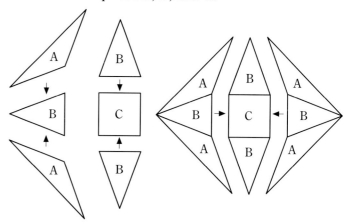

5. Add light chintz border, seaming strips as necessary and adding pieced corner squares. Follow the directions for "Borders with Corner Squares" on page 125.
6. Layer with batting and backing; quilt or tie. See page 133 for a quilting suggestion.
7. Bind with straight-grain or bias strips of fabric.

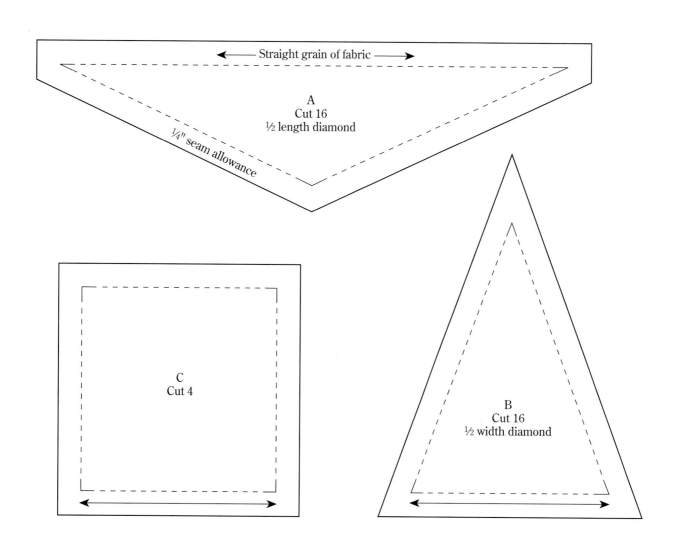

A
Cut 16
½ length diamond

←— Straight grain of fabric —→

¼" seam allowance

C
Cut 4

B
Cut 16
½ width diamond

Bridal Path

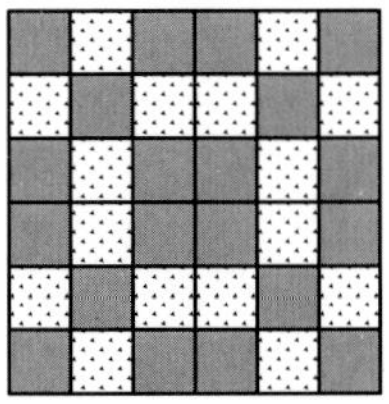

Block I
9" block

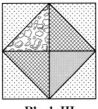

Block II
9" block

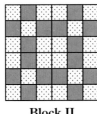

Block III
9" block

Dimensions: 51" x 63½"

32 blocks, 9" (6 Block I, 6 Block II, and 20 Block III), set on the diagonal; pieced side and corner setting triangles; finished without a border.

Materials: 44"-wide fabric

1½ yds. coral-print background fabric for Ninepatch units and side and corner setting triangles

6 fat quarters of assorted teal prints for Ninepatch blocks and side and corner setting triangles

5 fat quarters of assorted coral prints

1⅛ yds. light green fabric

3 yds. coordinating fabric for backing

½ yd. fabric for 234" of narrow binding

Batting and thread to finish

Cutting: All measurements include ¼" seams.

From the coral-print background fabric:

Cut 34 strips, 2" x 22", for Ninepatch blocks.

Cut 1 strip, 2" x 42". Cut strip into a total of 18 squares, 2" x 2", for pieced side and corner setting triangles.

Cut 1 strip, 3⅜" x 42". Cut strip into 12 squares, 3⅜" x 3⅜". Cut 2 additional squares, 3⅜" x 3⅜", from a scrap, for a total of 14 squares. Cut twice diagonally into 56 triangles. Use 54 for Corner Setting Triangle B and Side Setting Triangle B.

From the teal fat quarters:

Cut a total of 34 strips, 2" x 22", for Ninepatch blocks.

Cut a total of 18 squares, 2" x 2", for pieced side and corner setting triangles.

Cut a total of 14 squares, 3⅜" x 3⅜". Cut twice diagonally into 56 triangles. Use 54 for Corner Setting Triangle A and Side Setting Triangle A.

From each coral fat quarter:

Cut 8 squares, 5⅜" x 5⅜". Cut once diagonally into 16 triangles (80 total) for Block III.

From the light green fabric:

Cut 6 strips, 5⅜" x 42". Cut the strips into a total of 40 squares, 5⅜" x 5⅜". Cut once diagonally into 80 triangles for Block III.

DIRECTIONS

1. Join 2 of the 2" x 22" teal strips on either side of 1 of the 2" x 22" coral strips to make 10 strip units as shown. The units should measure 5" wide when sewn. Press seams toward the darker fabric. Cut the units into 93 segments, each 2" wide.

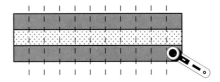

2. Join a 2" x 22" teal strip between 2 of the 2" x 22" coral strips to make 10 strip units as shown. The units should measure 5" wide when sewn. Cut the units into 93 segments, each 2" wide.

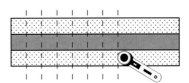

3. Stitch units together to make 31 Ninepatch blocks and 31 alternate Ninepatch blocks. Press for opposing seams.

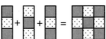 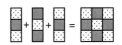

Ninepatch blocks   Alternate Ninepatch blocks

Opposing seams

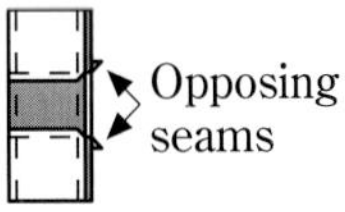

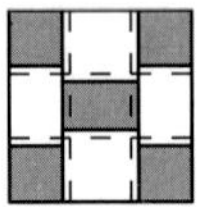

Pressing

4. Join Ninepatch blocks and alternate Ninepatch blocks into 6 of Block I and 6 of Block II. You will use the remaining segments in the pieced setting triangles.

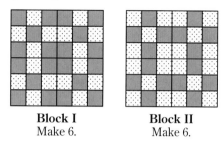

Block I
Make 6.

Block II
Make 6.

5. Join the coral and light green triangles to make 20 of Block III.

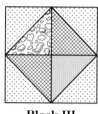

Block III
Make 20.

6. Join the remaining teal and coral strips to make 4 strip units as shown. The units should measure 3½" wide when sewn. Cut the units into 36 segments, each 2" wide.

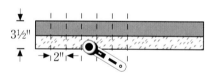

3½"

2"

7. Join these segments with the remaining segments from step 4 and the teal and coral squares and triangles to make 7 Side Setting Triangle A and 7 Side Setting Triangle B.

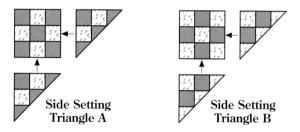

Side Setting Triangle A

Side Setting Triangle B

8. Join the remaining segments with the teal and coral squares and triangles to make 2 Corner

Setting Triangle A (for lower corners) and 2 Corner Setting Triangle B (for upper corners).

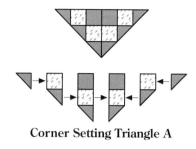

Corner Setting Triangle A

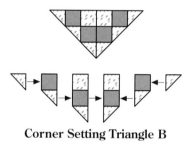

Corner Setting Triangle B

9. Join Blocks I, II, and III with the side and corner setting triangles to form the quilt top.

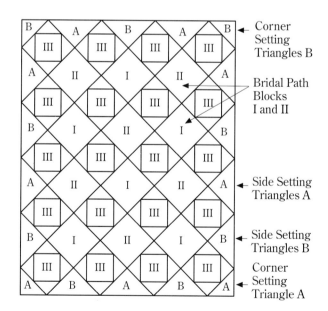

Corner Setting Triangles B

Bridal Path Blocks I and II

Side Setting Triangles A

Side Setting Triangles B

Corner Setting Triangle A

10. Layer with batting and backing; quilt or tie. See page 134 for a quilting suggestion.
11. Bind with straight-grain or bias strips of fabric.

Bridal Path *by Cleo Nollette, 1992, Seattle, Washington, 51" x 63½". Simple Ninepatch blocks in two color families form chains across the quilt top. The delicate coral fabrics showcase an assortment of teal prints. Quilted by Roxanne Carter. (Collection of That Patchwork Place, Inc.)*

Broken Dishes

Broken Dishes
5" block

Dimensions: 75" x 86"

240 blocks (120 Broken Dishes and 120 alternate), 5", set 15 across and 16 down; 3"-wide top and bottom border.

Note: One of the Broken Dishes blocks in the antique quilt pictured is turned "wrong." Was it deliberate? You can either duplicate or correct this "error" when you set your blocks together.

Materials: 44"-wide fabric

⅛ yd. each of 7 different red prints for Broken Dishes blocks
⅛ yd. each of 7 different light and/or medium blue prints for Broken Dishes blocks
⅛ yd. each of 8 different dark blue prints for Broken Dishes blocks
½ yd. each of 5 different light prints for Broken Dishes blocks
2⅞ yds. light print "A" for alternate blocks
½ yd. light print "B" for top and bottom border
5¼ yds. fabric for backing
¾ yd. fabric for 340" of narrow binding
Batting and thread to finish

Cutting: All measurements include ¼" seams.

From each red print:
Cut 1 strip, 3⅜" x 42", for a total of 7 strips. Cut the strips into 78 squares, 3⅜" x 3⅜". Cut once diagonally into 156 half-square triangles for Broken Dishes blocks.

From each light and/or medium blue print:
Cut 1 strip, 3⅜" x 42", for a total of 7 strips. Cut the strips into 74 squares, 3⅜" x 3⅜". Cut once diagonally into 148 half-square triangles for Broken Dishes blocks.

From each dark blue print:
Cut 1 strip, 3⅜" x 42", for a total of 8 strips. Cut the strips into 88 squares, 3⅜" x 3⅜". Cut once diagonally into 176 half-square triangles for Broken Dishes blocks.

From each of the 5 light prints:
Cut 4 strips, 3⅜" x 42", for a total of 20 strips. Cut the strips into 240 squares, 3⅜" x 3⅜". Cut once diagonally into 480 half-square triangles for Broken Dishes blocks.

From light print "A":
Cut 18 strips, 5½" x 42". Cut the strips into 120 squares, 5½" x 5½", for alternate blocks.

From light print "B":
Cut 4 strips, 3½" x 42", for top and bottom border.

DIRECTIONS

1. Join the red print half-square triangles and 156 of the light print half-square triangles to make 156 half-square triangle units. Join the half-square triangle units to make 39 Broken Dishes blocks, as shown.

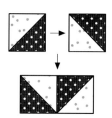

2. Join the light and/or medium blue print half-square triangles and 148 of the light print half-square triangles to make 148 half-square triangle units. Join the half-square triangle units to make 37 Broken Dishes blocks as shown above.

3. Join the dark blue print half-square triangles and the remaining light print half-square triangles to make 176 half-square triangle units. Join the half-square triangle units to make 44 Broken Dishes blocks as shown above.

4. Set the blocks together in rows of 15 as shown in the quilt photo, alternating Broken Dishes blocks and 5½" light print "A" squares; join the rows.

5. Add light print "B" top and bottom border, seaming strips as necessary.

6. Layer with batting and backing; quilt or tie. See page 134 for a quilting suggestion.

7. Bind with straight-grain or bias strips of fabric.

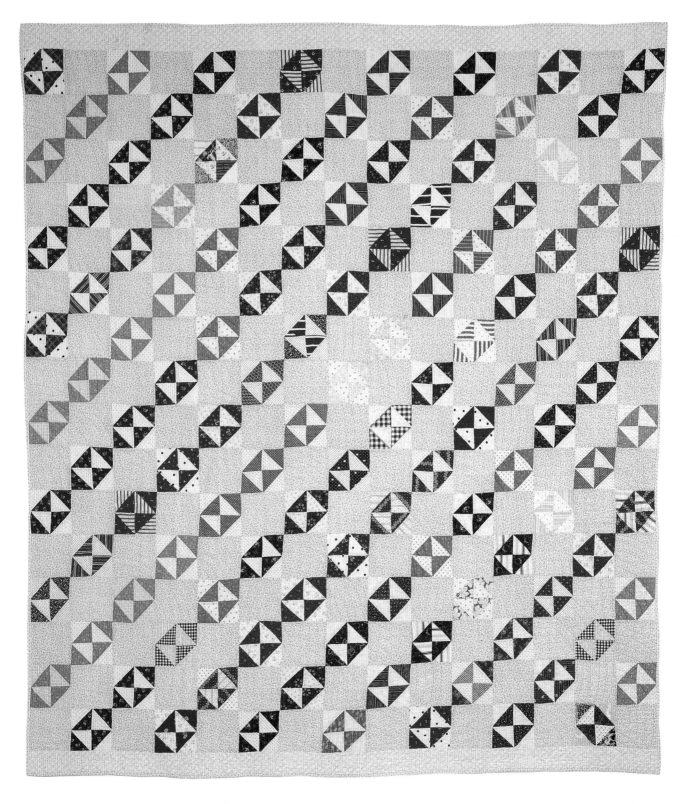

Broken Dishes, *maker unknown, c. 1930, purchased in Nebraska, 68″ x 78½″. The maker arranged her colors in tidy diagonal rows but interrupted the flow by turning one block the "wrong" way. Note: The pattern uses slightly larger blocks and produces a 75″ x 86″ quilt.*
(Collection of Rosie Huntemann)

Charm Quilt

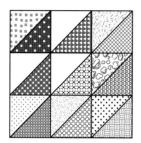

Charm Quilt
7½" block

Dimensions: 60" x 81¼"*

59 blocks, 7½", set on point 5 across and 7 down, floated with large setting triangles; finished without a border.

*Finished size will vary with size of setting triangles and trimming.

Note: In a charm quilt, no two fabrics are repeated. This quilt contains 1062 different triangles, which are rotary cut from scraps, using the ScrapSaver™ tool. (See "Multi-fabric Quilts from Scraps" on pages 25–27.)

Materials: 44"-wide fabric

Scraps large enough to cut 177 light, 354 medium, and 531 dark 3⅜" ScrapSaver triangles for blocks
2⅛ yds. dark brown print for setting triangles
3¾ yds. fabric for backing
⅝ yd. fabric for 301" of narrow binding
Batting and thread to finish

Cutting: All measurements include ¼" seams.

From the scraps:
Cut 177 light, 354 medium, and 531 dark 3⅜" ScrapSaver triangles, for blocks.

From the dark brown print:
Cut 5 squares, 19" x 19". Cut twice diagonally into 20 triangles for side set pieces.
Cut 2 squares, 13¼" x 13¼". Cut once diagonally into 4 triangles for corner setting pieces.

DIRECTIONS

1. Piece 59 blocks. Each block contains 9 dark, 6 medium, and 3 light triangles, arranged as shown below. In the pictured quilt, 16 of the blocks are primarily red, 16 are green, 14 are

blue, 5 are purple, 4 are brown, and 4 are black. If you don't have enough scraps of a particular color to duplicate the pictured quilt exactly, use browns, purples, or rusts in place of reds, or substitute greens or blacks for blues. Or, ignore color completely and concentrate on achieving the desired value distribution in the individual blocks. Just do the best you can with what you have and enjoy the wonderful results!

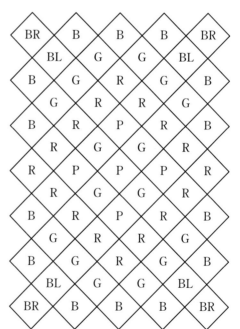

7½" block

2. Set the blocks together in diagonal rows with the dark brown side and corner setting triangles, arranging the colors as shown below. The setting triangles are cut large, to allow the blocks to "float." (See "Assembling On-Point Quilts" on pages 122–23.)

B = blue
BL = black
BR = brown
G = green
P = purple
R = red

3. Join the rows. Trim and square up the outside edges after the rows are sewn, if needed.
4. If desired, trim the corners of the quilt at a 45° angle as shown in the quilt photo.
5. Layer with batting and backing; quilt or tie. See page 134 for a quilting suggestion.
6. Bind with straight-grain or bias strips of fabric.

Charmed, I'm Sure *by Judy Hopkins, 1987, Anchorage, Alaska, 58" x 78½". Judy believes that the best way to become adept at combining printed fabrics is to make a charm quilt. This one includes 1064 different prints; Judy challenges her friends to find the one fabric that appears twice. Hint: It's blue.*

Chinese Puzzle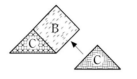

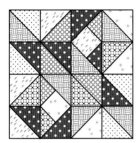

Chinese Puzzle
10" block

Dimensions: 31¼" x 43"

6 blocks, 10", set 2 across and 3 down with 1¾"-wide sashing and sashing squares; 3"-wide border.

Materials: 44"-wide fabric

6 fat quarters of assorted light background fabrics
6 fat quarters of assorted navy blue prints
½ yd. navy blue print for border
1⅜ yds. fabric for backing
⅜ yd. fabric for 152" of narrow binding
Batting and thread to finish

Cutting: All measurements include ¼" seams.

From each fat quarter of light background fabric:
Cut 2 squares, 2¼" x 2¼", for Piece B.
Cut 3 pieces, 2¼" x 10½", for sashing strips.

From each fat quarter of navy blue prints:
Cut 4 squares, 3⅜" x 3⅜". Cut once diagonally into 8 triangles (48 total) for Piece A.
Cut 1 square, 3¾" x 3¾". Cut twice diagonally into 4 triangles (24 total) for Piece C.
Cut 2 squares, 2¼" x 2¼", for sashing squares.

Cut the remainder of the light background and navy blue prints into 12" squares:
Divide into pairs; then cut and piece 2½"-wide bias strips, following the directions for bias squares on page 23. From this pieced fabric, cut 10 bias squares, 3" x 3".

From the navy blue print for border:
Cut 4 strips, 3¼" x 43½". If your fabric is less than 44" wide after preshrinking, you will need to cut an additional strip and piece the border to fit.

DIRECTIONS

1. Piece 12 of Unit I, using light background squares and navy blue triangles.

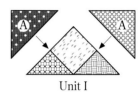

Unit I

2. Join 2 navy blue triangles (Piece A) to make 12 navy blue/navy blue bias squares.

3. Piece 6 Chinese Puzzle blocks, joining Unit I to both kinds of bias squares.

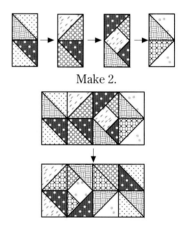

Make 2.

4. Join blocks into rows, using 2 blocks and 3 sashing strips.
5. Assemble 4 rows of sashing, using 2 sashing strips and 3 sashing squares.
6. Assemble rows of blocks with sashing between them as shown in the quilt photo.
7. Add navy blue border, seaming strips as necessary. See "Borders with Straight-Cut Corners" on page 124.
8. Layer with batting and backing; quilt or tie. See page 134 for a quilting suggestion.
9. Bind with straight-grain or bias strips of fabric.

Chinese Puzzle *by Nancy J. Martin, 1992, Woodinville, Washington, 31¼" x 43". Japanese kimono fabrics collected on a trip to Australia make this Chinese Puzzle pattern a true international quilt. The dark blue fabrics represent the two interlocking loops that are part of this age-old mind teaser. Quilted by Roxanne Carter. (Collection of That Patchwork Place, Inc.)*

City Lights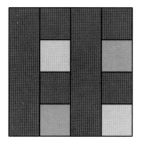

City Lights
8" block

Dimensions: 62" x 74"

20 blocks, 8", set 4 across and 5 down with 4"-wide sashing and pieced sashing squares; 1"-wide inner border, 4"-wide outer border.

Materials: 44"-wide fabric

2⅝ yds. black solid for blocks, pieced sashing squares, and outer border
1 strip, 2½" x 42", each of 8 different light solids (pinks, aquas, lavenders, light blues, light greens) for blocks and pieced sashing squares
1½ yds. medium blue print or solid for sashing
⅜ yd. purple solid for inner border
3⅞ yds. fabric for backing
⅝ yd. fabric for 290" of narrow binding
Batting and thread to finish

Cutting: All measurements include ¼" seams.

From the black solid:
Cut 10 strips, 4½" x 42". From 2 of the strips, cut a total of 30 segments, each 2½" wide, to make rectangles, 2½" x 4½", for pieced sashing squares. Leave the remaining 8 strips uncut, for outer border.
Cut 3 strips, 8½" x 42". Cut the strips into segments, each 2½" wide, to make 40 rectangles, each 2½" x 8½", for blocks.
Cut 8 strips, 2½" x 42", for blocks and pieced sashing squares.

From the medium blue print or solid:
Cut 6 strips, 8½" x 42". Cut the strips into segments, each 4½" wide, to make 49 rectangles, 4½" x 8½", for sashing.

From the purple solid:
Cut 8 strips, 1½" x 42", for inner border.

DIRECTIONS

1. Join any 6 of the 2½" x 42" light strips and 6 of the 2½" x 42" black strips to make 3 strip units as shown. The strip units should measure 8½" wide when sewn. Cut the units into a total of 40 segments, each 2½" wide.

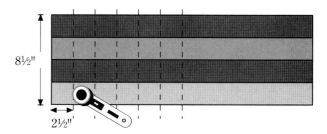

2. Join the segments with the 2½" x 8½" black rectangles to make 20 City Lights blocks as shown.

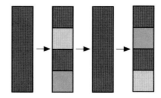

3. Join the remaining 2½" x 42" light and black strips to make 2 strip units as shown. The strip units should measure 4½" wide when sewn. Cut the units into a total of 30 segments, each 2½" wide.

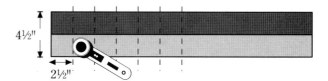

4. Join the segments with the 2½" x 4½" black rectangles to make 30 sashing squares as shown.

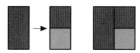

5. Set the blocks together with the 4½" x 8½" medium blue sashing pieces and the sashing squares as shown in the quilt photo.
6. Add purple inner border, seaming strips as necessary. See "Borders with Straight-Cut Corners" on page 124.
7. Add black outer border, as for inner border.
8. Layer with batting and backing; quilt or tie. See page 135 for a quilting suggestion.
9. Bind with straight-grain or bias strips of fabric.

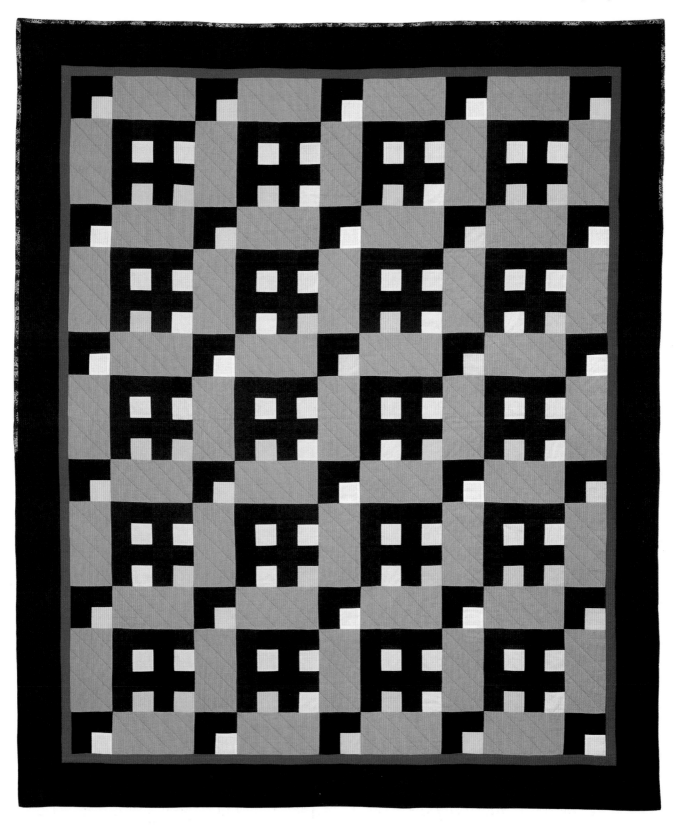

City Lights *by Jacquelin Carley, 1993, Anchorage, Alaska, 62" x 74". A Puss-in-a-Corner variation, Jackie's striking, cosmopolitan quilt is quick and easy to make and looks great in a variety of color combinations. Try it with fire-engine red sashing!*

Cleo's Castles in the Air

Cleo's Castles in the Air
9" block

Dimensions: 63" x 63"

16 blocks, 9", set 4 across and 4 down with 3"-wide sashing and sashing squares; 6"-wide border.

Materials: 44"-wide fabric

2 yds. blue-and-lavender print for block corners, sashing squares, and borders (cut lengthwise)
1 yd. blue paisley fabric for star background
½ yd. periwinkle blue fabric for small star tip
1½ yds. light blue print for star tips and sashing
Scraps of blue fabrics for star centers
3¾ yds. fabric for backing
½ yd. fabric for 260" of narrow binding
Batting and thread to finish

Cutting: All measurements include ¼" seams.

From the blue-and-lavender print:
Cut 2 strips, 3½" x 42". Cut the strips into 24 squares, 3½" x 3½". Cut 1 additional square from a scrap for a total of 25 sashing squares.
Cut 4 strips, each 6¼" wide, from the length of the fabric, for borders.

From the blue paisley and the remaining blue-and-lavender print:
Cut 2 fat quarters (approximately 18" x 22") from each of the fabrics. Pair each blue paisley fat quarter with a lavender print fat quarter; you will have 2 pairs. Cut and piece 3"-wide bias strips, following the directions for bias squares on page 23. From this pieced fabric, cut 64 bias squares, 3½" x 3½".

From the blue paisley and periwinkle blue fabrics:
Cut a fat quarter (18" x 22") from each of the fabrics. Layer, cut, and piece 3½"-wide bias strips, following the directions for bias squares on page 23. From this pieced fabric, cut 32 bias squares,

3⅞" x 3⅞". Cut once diagonally to make 64 of Unit .5 as shown on page 25.

From the remaining blue paisley fabric:
Cut 32 squares, 2⅜" x 2⅜". Cut once diagonally into 64 triangles for star centers.

From the light blue print:
Cut 4 strips, 3⅞" x 42". Cut strips into a total of 32 squares, 3⅞" x 3⅞". Cut once diagonally into 64 triangles for star tips.
Cut 10 strips, 3½" x 42". Cut strips into a total of 40 pieces, 3½" x 9½", for sashing strips.

From the scraps of blue fabrics:
Cut 16 squares, 2⅝" x 2⅝", for star centers.

DIRECTIONS

1. Piece 16 star centers, using the 2⅝" blue squares and the blue paisley triangles.

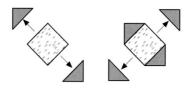

2. Join Unit .5 to light blue triangles. You will have 32 of each configuration.

Unit .5   Alternate Unit .5

3. Piece 16 Cleo's Castles in the Air blocks, using the star centers, identical units of Unit .5, and bias squares. In 8 of the blocks, you will use one type of Unit .5, and in 8 you will use the alternate Unit .5.

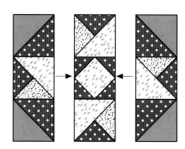 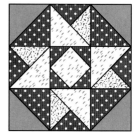

Alternate configuration

4. Join blocks into rows, using 4 blocks (alternate configuration) and 5 sashing strips.

5. Assemble 5 rows of sashing, using 4 sashing strips and 5 sashing squares.

6. Join rows of blocks with sashing between them as shown in the photo.

7. Add blue and lavender print border, seaming strips as necessary. See "Borders with Straight-Cut Corners" on page 124.

8. Layer with batting and backing; quilt or tie. See page 135 for a quilting suggestion.

9. Bind with straight-grain or bias strips of fabric.

Cleo's Castles in the Air *by Nancy J. Martin, 1992, Woodinville, Washington, 63" x 63". Delicate blue fabrics highlight the white center stars, which appear to spin in two directions. A Baptist Fan pattern was quilted in the border. Quilted by Marta Estes. (Collection of That Patchwork Place, Inc.)*

Double Irish Chain

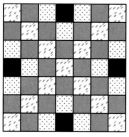

Double Irish Chain
10½" block

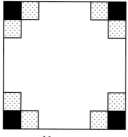

Alternate
10½" block

Dimensions: 75" x 75"

36 blocks (18 Chain blocks and 18 alternate), 10½", set 6 across and 6 down; 6"-wide border.

Materials: 44"-wide fabric

2 yds. of assorted black prints for alternate blocks
1½ yds. assorted indigo blue prints for Chain blocks
2 yds. light checked, striped, or print fabrics for Chain and alternate blocks
¾ yd. of assorted black background fabrics for Chain blocks and corners of alternate blocks
1½ yds. black background fabric for border
4½ yds. fabric for backing
⅝ yd. fabric for 300" of narrow binding
Batting and thread to finish

Cutting: All measurements include ¼" seams.

Note: Corner squares of the alternate blocks were cut separately and appliquéd in place, so the checks and prints of the background squares were not interrupted by seams.

From the black prints for alternate blocks:
　　Cut 18 squares, 11" x 11".

From the indigo blue prints:
　　Cut 20 strips, 2" x 42", for Chain blocks.

From the light checked, striped, or print fabrics:
　　Cut 25 strips, 2" x 42", for Chain blocks.
　　Cut 144 squares, 2" x 2", for alternate blocks.

From the black background fabrics for Chain and alternate blocks:
　　Cut 4 strips, 2" x 42", for Chain blocks.
　　Cut 72 squares, 2" x 2", for corners of alternate blocks.

From the black background fabric for border:
　　Cut 8 strips, 6¼" x 42".

DIRECTIONS

1. Join the 2" x 42" strips into units as shown. Make 2 each of Units I, II, and III, and 1 of Unit IV. The units should measure 11" wide when sewn. Cut each strip into 18 segments, each 2" wide.

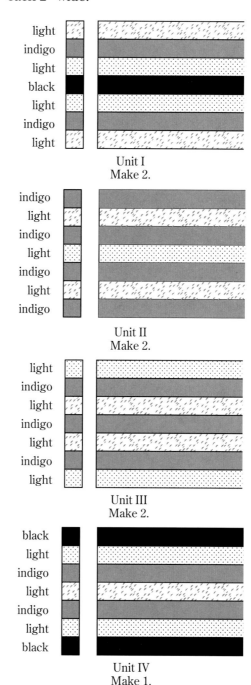

light
indigo
light
black
light
indigo
light

Unit I
Make 2.

indigo
light
indigo
light
indigo
light
indigo

Unit II
Make 2.

light
indigo
light
indigo
light
indigo
light

Unit III
Make 2.

black
light
indigo
light
indigo
light
black

Unit IV
Make 1.

2. Appliqué the black background squares onto the corners of the alternate blocks. Appliqué 2

squares of light checked, striped, or print fabric to each corner.

3. Join together in rows of 6 blocks, alternating the blocks. Join rows together as shown in the quilt photo

4. Add black-background border, seaming strips as necessary. See "Borders with Straight-Cut Corners" on page 124.
5. Layer with batting and backing; quilt or tie. See page 135 for a quilting suggestion.
6. Bind with straight-grain or bias strips of fabric.

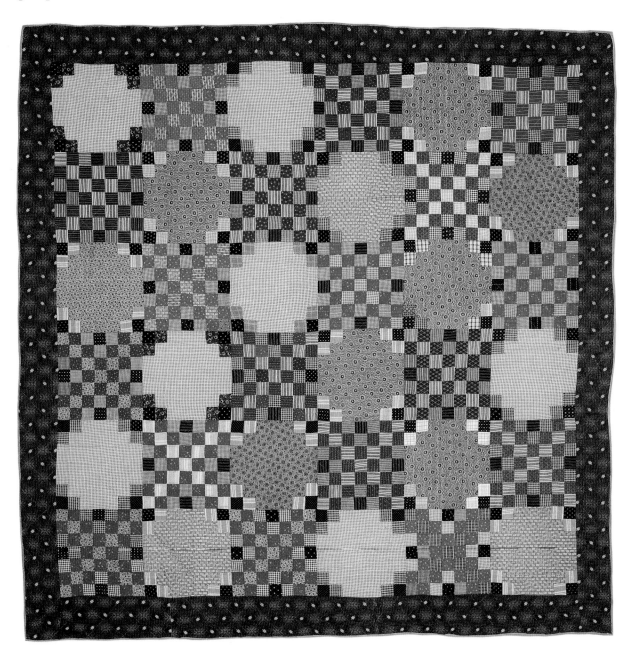

Double Irish Chain, *maker unknown, c. 1900, Pennsylvania, 75″ x 75″. Dark indigo prints contrast with checks and stripes in this Irish Chain quilt. The dark checks and Shaker gray prints used in the alternate blocks give a masculine feel to this quilt. (Collection of Nancy J. Martin)*

Double Wrench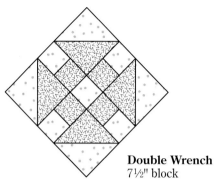

Double Wrench
7½" block

Dimensions: 64" x 85"

83 blocks, 7½", set on point 6 across and 8 down; finished without a border.

Materials: 44"-wide fabric

4 yards muslin or light print for blocks and setting triangles

4¼" x 13" pieces of 83 different medium and/or dark fabrics for blocks (Nearest cut is ⅛ yd.)

5⅛ yds. fabric for backing

⅝ yd. fabric for 316" of narrow binding

Batting and thread to finish

Cutting: All measurements include ¼" seams.

From the muslin or light print:

Cut 17 strips, 3⅞" x 42". Cut the strips into a total of 166 squares, 3⅞" x 3⅞". Cut once diagonally into 332 triangles for blocks.

Cut 20 strips, 2" x 42". Cut the strips into a total of 415 squares, 2" x 2", for blocks.

Cut 6 squares, 11⅞" x 11⅞". Cut twice diagonally into 24 triangles for side setting pieces.

Cut 2 squares, 6¼" x 6¼". Cut once diagonally into 4 triangles for corner setting pieces.

From each of the 4¼" x 13" scraps:

Cut 2 squares, 3⅞" x 3⅞". Cut once diagonally into 4 triangles for blocks.

Cut 4 squares, 2" x 2", for blocks.

DIRECTIONS

1. Piece 83 Double Wrench blocks as shown. Each block is made by combining muslin or light print pieces with pieces cut from one of the 83 medium or dark scraps.

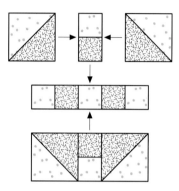

2. Set the blocks together in diagonal rows with the muslin or light print side and corner triangles. See "Assembling On-Point Quilts" on pages 122–23. Join the rows as shown in the quilt photo. Trim and square up the outside edges after the rows are sewn, if needed.
3. Layer with batting and backing; quilt or tie. See page 135 for a quilting suggestion.
4. Bind with straight-grain or bias strips of fabric.

Fields of Calico *by Louise Pease, 1992, Anchorage, Alaska, 83" x 111". Double Wrench blocks set on point form an intriguing secondary dot-dash pattern. Each of the 83 blocks was made from a different fabric. Note: The pattern uses smaller blocks and produces a 64" x 85" quilt.*

Fine Feathered Star ■■■

Feathered Star
19" block

Dimensions: 80½" x 80½"

9 blocks, 19", set as a bar quilt with 3 stars across and 3 down; 1¾"-wide 1st border, 2"-wide pieced 2nd border, 2"-wide 3rd border, and a 6"-wide 4th border.

Materials: 44"-wide fabric

4⅞ yds. tone-on-tone print for background of bias squares, unit pieces, and borders
9 contrasting fat quarters for star feathers and tips
9 dark blue fat quarters for star centers and large triangles
2¼ yds. dark blue print for outer border
4¾ yds. fabric for backing
¾ yd. fabric for 360" of narrow binding
Batting and thread to finish

Cutting: All measurements include ¼" seams.

From the tone-on-tone background print:

Cut 9 fat quarters, each 18" x 22". Pair each with a contrasting fat quarter of fabric; then cut into 2 sets, each 11" x 18". Use 1 set to cut and piece 1¾"-wide bias strips, following the directions for bias squares on page 23. For each star, cut 24 large bias squares, 1⁹⁄₁₆" x 1⁹⁄₁₆" (or use Template B on page 143), from matching fabrics, and 24 small bias squares, 1½" x 1½" (or use Template A on page 143). Be sure to keep these two sizes of bias squares separated.

Use the remaining 11" x 18" sets to cut the star tips, small triangles, and squares. Cut 4 squares, 1⁹⁄₁₆" x 1⁹⁄₁₆", from the remainder of each contrasting fat quarter for Piece B.

For a quick method for cutting star tips and small triangles, see the Tip Box on page 60, or use Templates C and G on page 143.

From the remaining tone-on-tone background print:

Cut 4 squares, 6⅛" x 6⅛", for Unit III.
Cut 8 rectangles, 6⅛" x 11½", for Unit IV.
Cut 4 squares, 11½" x 11½", for Unit V.
Cut 12 squares, 6⅛" x 6⅛", for Piece E.
Cut 3 squares, 9¼" x 9¼", for Piece F. Cut twice diagonally into 12 triangles.
Cut 4 squares, 1⅞" x 1⅞". Cut once diagonally into 8 triangles for Piece H.
Cut 8 strips, 2¼" x 42", for 1st border.
Cut 8 strips, 2½" x 42", for 3rd border.

From each of the dark blue fat quarters:

Cut 1 square, 8½" x 8½", for star center (Unit I).
Cut 4 squares, 3⅞" x 3⅞". Cut once diagonally into 8 triangles (72 total) for Piece D.

From the dark blue print for outer border:

Cut 4 strips, 6¼" x 80".

DIRECTIONS

To avoid seams through the large areas of background fabric, construct this quilt in units as a bar quilt. (See pages 123–24.) After joining units into rows, stars appear as quilt is set together.

1. Piece 12 of Unit VI, using templates as labeled and following the piecing diagram as a guide. Take care to match fabrics for feathers and tips on each star.

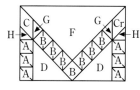 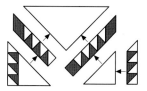

2. Piece 12 of Unit II, using templates on page 143 as labeled and following the piecing diagram as a guide. As you piece the units, arrange the feathers and tips so that the fabrics match on each star.

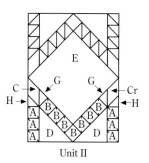 

Unit II

Fine Feathered Star *by Nancy J. Martin, 1992, Woodinville, Washington, 80½" x 80½".*
A traditional Feathered Star design is enhanced by a magnificent collection of
reproduction chintzes. The sawtooth border and exquisite quilting stitches by Alvina Nelson
create an energetic, appealing quilt. (Collection of That Patchwork Place, Inc.)

3. Join completed units to form rows. Join rows as shown:

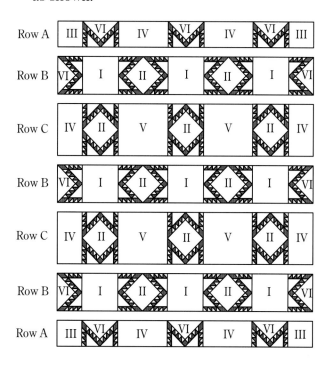

4. Add tone-on-tone 1st border, seaming strips as necessary. See "Borders with Straight-Cut Corners" on page 124. The quilt should now measure 60½" x 60½".

5. Add Sawtooth border of 2½" x 2½" bias squares. Each border has 30 bias squares on each side, 15 facing each direction and a 2½" square of background fabric in each corner.

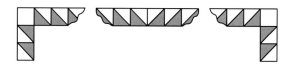

6. Add tone-on-tone 3rd border, as for inner border.
7. Add dark blue 4th border, as for previous border.
8. Layer with batting and backing; quilt or tie. See page 136 for a quilting suggestion.
9. Bind with straight-grain or bias strips of fabric.

TIP
Triangle-Parallelogram Units (Star Tips)

From each of the remaining sets of 11" x 18" fabrics, cut and piece together 1 set of three 1¾"-wide bias strips with the dark fabric on the outside edge.

1. Place the diagonal line of the Bias Square ruler on the seam line, and the 1⁹⁄₁₆" ruler measurement on the bottom edge. Use Template B on page 143 to check your measurement. Cut the first two sides of the unit (1) so that a parallelogram is attached to the triangle.

2. Even up the bottom edge by cutting a 1⁹⁄₁₆" bias square as shown. Discard or save for another project.
3. Cut the next unit (2) by placing the Bias Square 1⁹⁄₁₆" beyond the previous cut.
4. The next unit (3) you cut will be a reverse unit. Align the diagonal line on the seam and the 1⁹⁄₁₆" ruler measurement on the left edge of the dark strip. Trim the excess white fabric from the left side of the unit.
5. Continue cutting the remaining star tips, reversing the direction of each cut until you have 4 regular units and 4 reverse units (4-8). Discard the extra regular unit. Trim excess fabric as necessary.

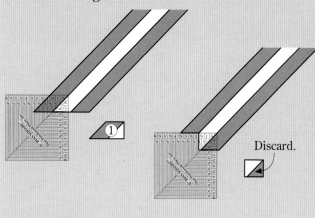

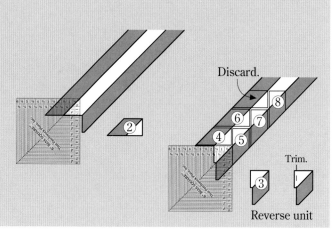

Four Corners

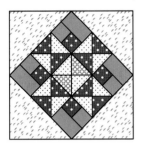

Four Corners
12 ³/₄"

Dimensions: 52" x 52"

9 blocks, 12¾", set 3 across and 3 down; 4¾"-wide pieced inner border and 2"-wide outer border.

Materials: 44"-wide fabric

1½ yds. assorted light prints for stars and pieced inner border
1½ yds. assorted black prints for stars and pieced inner border
1½ yds. assorted tan and taupe fabrics for star corners and block corners
⅝ yd. medium fabric for outer border
3 yds. fabric for backing
½ yd. fabric for 210" of narrow binding
Batting and thread to finish

Cutting: All measurements include ¼" seams.

From the assorted light and black prints:

For the bias squares, cut 6 light and 6 dark pieces of fabric, each 10" x 10". Layer in pairs and cut into 3½"-wide bias strips, following the directions for making bias squares on page 23.

From this pieced fabric, cut 45 bias squares, 3⅞" x 3⅞". Stack 2 bias squares, with seam allowances opposing, and cut once diagonally. Resew in pairs to make 45 Square Two units. (See page 25.)

From the remaining black prints:

Cut 36 squares, 2" x 2", for star corners.
Cut 17 squares, 6" x 6". Cut twice diagonally into 68 triangles for pieced border.

From the remaining light prints:

Cut 15 squares, 6" x 6". Cut twice diagonally into 60 triangles for the pieced border.
Cut 4 and 4r from Border Template 1, found on page 62, for pieced border corners.

From the assorted tan and taupe fabrics:

Cut 36 squares, 2" x 2", for star corners.

Cut 36 pieces, 2" x 3½", for star corners.
Cut 18 squares (2 matching for each block), 7½" x 7½". Cut once diagonally into 36 triangles.

From the medium fabric for outer border:

Cut 8 strips, 2¼" x 42".

DIRECTIONS

1. Piece 9 Four Corners blocks, using the Square Two units and corner pieces. Each "star" in the Four Corners blocks should have 4 matching Square Two units and an alternate coloration in the center. Trim blocks to 13¼".

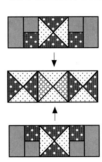 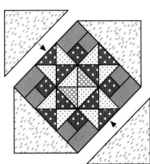

2. Join 3 blocks in a row. Stitch rows together as shown in the quilt photo.

3. Join 9 dark triangles and 8 light triangles in a row for inner section of the pieced border. Join 8 dark and 7 light triangles, adding light print border corners at each end of the strip for the outer section of the pieced border.

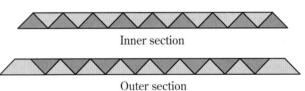

Inner section

Outer section

4. Join the two sections of the pieced inner border as shown. Then add the outer border to form a finished border strip for each side, top, and bottom.

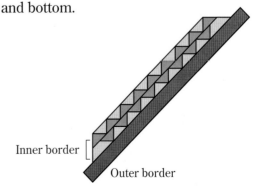

Inner border
Outer border

5. Stitch the finished borders to the quilt, stopping ¼" from outer edges. Miter the corners as shown on page 125.

6. Layer with batting and backing; quilt or tie. See page 136 for a quilting suggestion.

7. Bind with straight-grain or bias strips of fabric.

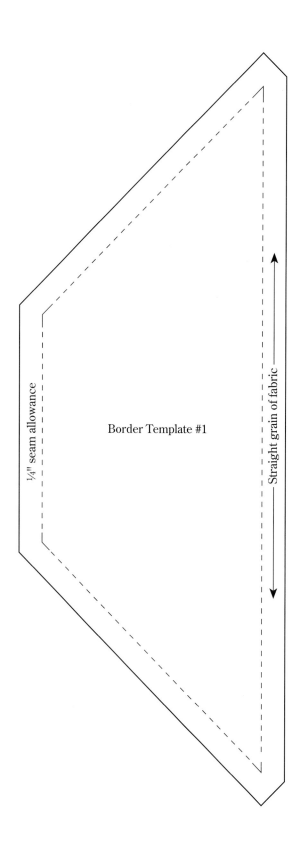

Border Template #1

¼" seam allowance

Straight grain of fabric

Four Corners *by Nancy J. Martin, 1992, Woodinville, Washington, 52" x 52". Black-and-white stars, set off by tan and taupe fabrics, emerge in the center of each Four Corners block. Black fabrics create an effective zigzag border surrounding the blocks. Quilted by Donna K. Gundlach. (Collection of That Patchwork Place, Inc.)*

Hearts and Hourglass

Hourglass
4" block

Heart
4" block

Dimensions: 68" x 92"

391 blocks (288 Hourglass and 103 appliqué Heart blocks), 4", set 17 across and 23 down; finished without a border.

Materials: 44"-wide fabric

1⅔ yds. muslin or light background print for appliqué heart backgrounds
1¼ yds. total or 103 squares, 4", assorted red, blue, and brown prints or solids for appliqué hearts
4¼ yds. total or 36 squares, 12", assorted light and light-medium prints for Hourglass blocks
4¼ yds. total or 36 squares, 12", assorted medium and dark prints, predominantly reds, blues, and browns for Hourglass blocks
5½ yds. fabric for backing
¾ yd. fabric for 338" of narrow binding
Batting and thread to finish

Cutting: All measurements include ¼" seams.

From the muslin or light background print:
Cut 12 strips, 4½" x 42". Cut the strips into a total of 103 squares, 4½" x 4½", for Heart backgrounds.

From the assorted light and light-medium prints:
Cut 36 squares, 12" x 12", for bias strip piecing for Hourglass blocks.

From the assorted medium and dark prints:
Cut 36 squares, 12" x 12", for bias strip piecing for Hourglass blocks.

DIRECTIONS

1. Use the template on page 143 to make 103 bond-paper or freezer-paper hearts as shown on page 29. Pin the paper patches to the wrong side of the 4" assorted red, blue, and brown squares; cut out hearts, adding ¼" seam allowance. Turn the seam allowance over the edge of the paper patch and press or baste.
2. Appliqué a heart to each of the 4½" muslin or light background print squares. (See "Appliqué" on pages 29–30.)
3. To make Hourglass blocks, place one of the 12" light or light-medium squares and one of the 12" medium or dark squares together right sides up to cut at the same time. Cut diagonally, corner to corner, to establish the bias, then cut bias strips 4¼" wide. You will have 2 sets of strips plus 4 corner triangles.

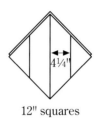
12" squares

4. Stitch bias strips and corner triangles together to make 2 strip-pieced units. Press all seams toward the darker fabric.

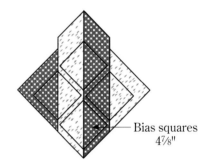
Bias squares 4⅞"

5. Use the Bias Square ruler to cut 8 bias squares, each 4⅞" x 4⅞", from the strip-pieced units.
6. Match pairs of the 4⅞" bias squares, right sides together, nesting opposing seams. Cut once diagonally and join the resulting triangle pairs to make 8 Hourglass blocks.
7. Repeat the above steps with the remaining 12" squares. When you have cut and stitched all 72 squares, you will have a total of 288 Hourglass blocks.
8. Set the Hourglass and appliqué Heart blocks together in rows of 17 as shown in the quilt photo. Note that the center blocks are arranged to form a small star-and-heart medallion with the hearts turned in various directions. Join the rows.
9. Layer with batting and backing; quilt or tie. See page 137 for a quilting suggestion.
10. Bind with straight-grain or bias strips of fabric.

Hearts and Hourglass *by Sarah Kaufman, 1991, West Linn, Oregon, 72" x 96". This is an adaptation of an early nineteenth-century quilt. The blocks are arranged to form a small star-and-heart medallion in the center. Note: The pattern uses slightly smaller blocks and produces a 68" x 92" quilt.*

Humble Homes

Humble Homes
10" block

Dimensions: 86" x 110"

48 blocks, 10", set 6 across and 8 down with
2"-wide sashing and sashing squares; 2"-wide inner
border; 6"-wide outer border.

Materials: 44"-wide fabric

1½ yds. assorted light checked, striped, and print
  fabrics for windows
1½ yds. assorted dark checked, striped, and print
  fabrics for roofs
2½ yds. assorted red, navy blue, blue, or gray
  fabrics for houses and doors
1¾ yds. assorted light blue fabrics for sky
Scraps of red, blue, or gray prints for chimneys
¼ yd. plaid fabric for sashing squares
2¼ yds. medium blue fabric for sashing and inner
  border
2 yds. dark blue fabric for outer border
7½ yds. fabric for backing
¾ yd. fabric for 400" of narrow binding
Batting and thread to finish

Cutting: All measurements include ¼" seams.

Note: The cutting directions for windows and
house pieces are given in sets, since all windows
and house pieces match within each block.

**From the assorted light checked, striped, and print
fabrics for windows, cut 48 sets of the following:**
  Cut 5 squares, 2½" x 2½", for each house.

**From the assorted dark checked, striped, and print
fabrics for roofs:**
  Cut 48 pieces, 3½" x 10½". Use Trimming
Template on page 143 to cut corner angles of
roofs.

**From the assorted red, navy blue, blue, or gray
fabrics for houses, cut 48 sets of the following,
matching grain lines of stripes and checks as shown**

in the illustration below:
  Cut 4 strips, 1½" x 2½" (lengthwise grain).
  Cut 4 strips, 1½" x 3½" (lengthwise grain).
  Cut 2 strips, 1½" x 2½" (crosswise grain).
  Cut 1 strip, 1½" x 10½" (crosswise grain).

From the remaining red, navy blue, and blue prints:
  Cut 48 pieces, 2½" x 3½", for doors.

**From the light blue fabrics for sky, cut 48 sets of
the following:**
  Cut 2 strips, 1½" x 2½".
  Cut 1 piece each from Template #1 and #1r on
page 143.
  Cut 1 piece, 1½" x 4½".

From the scraps of prints for chimneys:
  Cut 96 squares, 1½" x 1½" (48 matching sets).

From the plaid fabric for sashing squares:
  Cut 35 squares, 2½" x 2½".

From the medium blue fabric for sashing:
  Cut 10 strips, 2½" x 42" for inner border.
  Cut 82 pieces, 2½" x 10½".

From the dark blue fabric for outer border:
  Cut 10 strips, 6¼" x 42".

DIRECTIONS

1. Piece 48 Humble Homes blocks, matching
   grain lines of plaids and stripes.

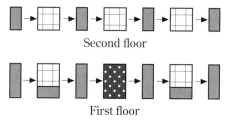

Second floor

First floor

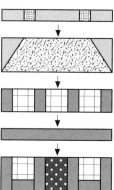

2. Join blocks into rows, using 6 blocks and 5 sashing strips for each row.
3. Assemble 7 rows of sashing, using 6 sashing strips and 5 sashing squares.
4. Assemble rows of blocks with rows of sashing between as shown in the quilt plan.
5. Add medium blue inner border, seaming strips as necessary. See "Borders with Straight-Cut Corners" on page 124.
6. Add the dark blue outer border, as for inner border.
7. Layer with batting and backing; quilt or tie. See page 137 for a quilting suggestion.
8. Bind with straight-grain or bias strips of fabric.

Humble Homes *by Mariet Soethout, 1989, Amsterdam, Netherlands, 86″ x 110″. Stripe, plaid, and checked fabrics form graphic houses, which represent typical Dutch dwellings. (Photo courtesy of* den haan *and* wagenmakers.*)*

Jack-in-the-Box

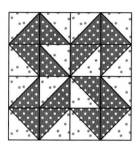

Jack-in-the-Box
10" block

Dimensions: 82" x 92"

56 blocks, 10", set 7 across and 8 down; 6"-wide border.

Materials: 44"-wide fabric

18 fat quarters of assorted light fabrics in white, pink, or checks
18 fat quarters of assorted dark fabrics in red, blue, or black
2 yds. black fabric for border
5½ yds. fabric for backing
⅝ yd. fabric for 360" of narrow binding
Batting and thread to finish

Cutting: All measurements include ¼" seams.

From the light and dark fat quarters:
Pair light and dark fat quarters and cut into 2¾"-wide bias strips, following the directions for making bias squares on page 23. From this pieced fabric, cut 896 bias squares, 3" x 3".

From the black fabric for border:
Cut 10 strips, 6¼" x 42".

DIRECTIONS

1. Piece 56 Jack-in-the-Box blocks. Note in the photo on page 69 that not all the blocks have matching fabrics within the bias squares.

Make 4.   Make 4.

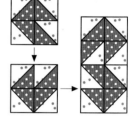

Join.

2. Join blocks together in rows of 7 blocks.
3. Join rows together to form quilt top.
4. Add black border, seaming strips as necessary. See "Borders with Straight-Cut Corners" on page 124.
5. Layer with batting and backing; quilt or tie. See page 137 for a quilting suggestion.
6. Bind with straight-grain or bias strips of fabric.

Jack-in-the-Box, *origin unknown, c. 1923, Colorado, 82" x 92". This lively scrap quilt is energized by the striped and checked fabrics that are randomly placed across the quilt top. Quilted by Beverly Payne. (Collection of That Patchwork Place, Inc.)*

Market Square

Market Square
16" block

Dimensions: 76" x 76"

16 blocks, 16", set 4 across and 4 down; 6"-wide border.

Materials: 44"-wide fabric

8 fat quarters of assorted light background fabrics
2⅝ yds. assorted purple fabrics
⅝ yd. red bandanna fabric or 3 bandannas
1¼ yds. assorted chintz large-scale prints for block centers
1½ yds. purple fabric for border
4½ yds. fabric for backing
⅝ yd. fabric for 314" of narrow binding
Batting and thread to finish

Cutting: All measurements include ¼" seams.

From 5 light background fabrics:
Cut 5 fat quarters (18" x 22") from purple background fabric and pair with 5 fat quarters of light background fabric. Layer and cut 2½"-wide bias strips, following the directions for making bias squares on page 23. From this pieced fabric, cut 256 bias squares, 2½" x 2½".

From the remaining fat quarters of light background fabric:
Cut 96 squares, 2⅞" x 2⅞". Cut once diagonally into 192 triangles.

From the remaining purple fabrics:
Cut 16 squares, 6⅞" x 6⅞". Cut once diagonally into 32 triangles for block corners.
Cut 96 squares, 2⅞" x 2⅞". Cut once diagonally into 192 triangles.

From the red bandanna fabric:
Cut 16 squares, 6⅞" x 6⅞". Cut once diagonally into 32 triangles for block corners.

From the assorted chintz large-scale prints:
Cut 16 squares, 9" x 9", for block centers.

From the purple fabric for border:
Cut 8 strips, 6¼" x 42".

DIRECTIONS

1. Piece 16 Market Square blocks. Use red corner triangles on 8 blocks and purple corner triangles on the other 8 blocks.

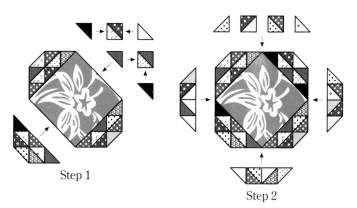

Step 1

Step 2

2. Join blocks together in rows of 4 blocks.
3. Join rows together to form the quilt top.
4. Add purple border, seaming strips as necessary. See "Borders with Straight-Cut Corners" on page 124.
5. Layer with batting and backing; quilt or tie. See page 138 for a quilting suggestion.
6. Bind with straight-grain or bias strips of fabric.

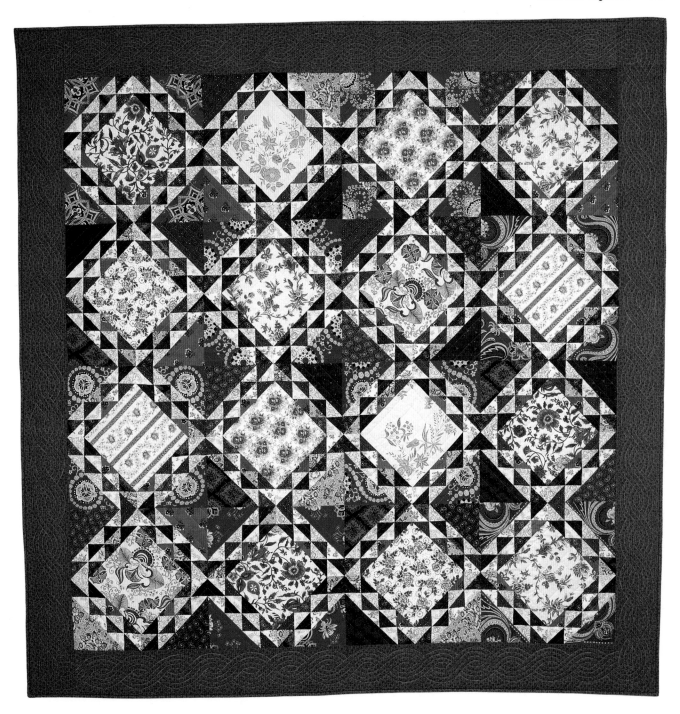

Market Square *by Nancy J. Martin, 1992, Woodinville, Washington, 76" x 76". This quilt was named for the central square, where one finds the town hall, town clock, and open-air markets, in the villages of Holland and Belgium. The fabrics were purchased in the Netherlands and represent the variety of people who congregate in the market square: i.e., purple antique fabrics for the widows who observe the traditional mourning period, and red triangles cut from bandannas for the younger women. The light background fabrics used in the small triangles were cut from traditional bedding fabrics, while the large squares feature both antique and reproduction chintz fabrics used in costumes of the various villages. Quilted by Sue von Jentzen. (Collection of That Patchwork Place, Inc.)*

Memory Wreath

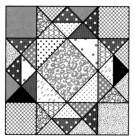

Memory Wreath
12" block

Dimensions: 71½" x 85½"

20 blocks, 12", set 4 across and 5 down with 2"-wide sashing; 1¾"-wide inner border and 5"-wide outer border.

Materials: 44"-wide fabric

12 fat quarters of assorted red fabrics for center, star tips, and sashing
5 fat quarters of assorted tan fabrics
4 fat quarters of assorted navy blue fabrics
5 fat quarters of assorted green fabrics
¼ yd. plaid fabric for sashing squares
⅝ yd. navy blue fabric for inner border
1⅜ yds. fabric for outer border*
5 yds. fabric for backing
⅝ yd. fabric for 314" of narrow binding
Batting and thread to finish

*Purchase 2½ yds. striped fabric to make a mitered border that resembles a frame to duplicate the border shown in the photo on page 73.

Cutting: All measurements include ¼" seams.

From 2 red and 2 tan fat quarters:
    Pair red and tan fat quarters and cut into 2½"-wide bias strips, following the directions for making bias squares on page 23. Piece together strips and cut 40 bias squares, 2⅝" x 2⅝".

From 4 red and 4 navy blue fat quarters:
    Pair red and navy blue fabrics. Cut and piece 3½"-wide bias strips, following the directions for making bias squares on page 23. Cut 80 bias squares, 3⅞" x 3⅞". Cut these bias squares in half diagonally to make 160 of Unit .5. (See page 25.)

From the remaining red fat quarters:
    Cut 20 squares, 4¾" x 4¾", for centers.
    Cut 49 strips, 2½" x 12½", for sashing.

From the remaining tan fat quarters:
    Cut 40 squares, 3⅞" x 3⅞". Cut once diagonally into 80 triangles.

From the green fat quarters:
    Cut 80 squares, 3½" x 3½", for corners.
    Cut 40 squares, 4¼" x 4¼". Cut twice diagonally into 160 triangles for outside edges.

From the plaid fabric:
    Cut 2 strips, 2½" x 42". Cut into a total of 30 sashing squares, 2½" x 2½".

From the navy blue fabric for inner border:
    Cut 8 strips, 2¼" x 42".

From the fabric for outer border:
    Cut 2 strips, 5¼" x 74", along the lengthwise grain of the fabric.
    Cut 2 strips, 5¼" x 88", along the lengthwise grain of the fabric.

Note: Cut 8 strips, 5¼" x 42", if you choose not to use striped fabric.

DIRECTIONS

1. Piece 20 Memory Wreath blocks as shown.

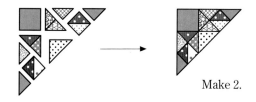

Make 2.

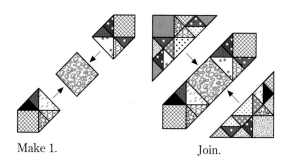

Make 1.   Join.

2. Join 4 blocks and 5 sashing strips into a row. Make 5 rows.
3. Join 5 sashing squares and 4 sashing strips together. Make 6 of these.
4. Join rows of blocks with sashing strips as shown in the quilt photo.

5. Join strips for inner and outer borders together, then sew to the quilt top, mitering the corners as shown on page 125.

6. Layer with batting and backing; quilt or tie. See page 138 for a quilting suggestion.

7. Bind with straight-grain or bias strips of fabric.

Memory Wreath *by Nancy J. Martin, 1992, Woodinville, Washington, 71½" x 85½". This scrappy quilt has a traditional color scheme that features a collection of patriotic prints. A dark, swirling paisley border surrounds and calms the interior blocks. Quilted by Hazel Montague. (Collection of That Patchwork Place, Inc.)*

Milky Way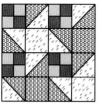

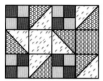

Milky Way
12" block

Right side unit
9" x 12"
Make 5.

Bottom unit
9" x 12"
Make 5.

Corner unit
9" x 9"
Make 1 for lower right.

Dimensions: 69" x 69"

25 blocks, 12", set 5 across and 5 down with side, bottom, and corner units; finished without a border.

Materials: 44"-wide fabric

9 fat quarters of navy blue prints with light
   background
9 fat quarters of dark navy blue prints
4 fat quarters of purple fabric for Four Patch units
1 yd. light blue fabric for Four Patch units
4 yds. fabric for backing
½ yd. fabric for 280" of narrow binding
Batting and thread to finish

Cutting: All measurements include ¼" seams.

From the fat quarters of navy blue prints with light background:
   Cut 61 squares (total), 3½" x 3½".
   Cut 121 squares (total), 3⅞" x 3⅞". Cut once diagonally into 242 triangles.

From the navy blue fat quarters:
   Cut 60 squares (total), 3½" x 3½".
   Cut 121 squares (total), 3⅞" x 3⅞". Cut once diagonally into 242 triangles.

From the purple fat quarters:
   Cut 30 strips, 2" x 22", for Four Patch units.

From the light blue fabric:
   Cut 30 strips, 2" x 22", for Four Patch units..

DIRECTIONS

1. Make 144 Four Patch units to use in blocks. Sew purple and light blue 2" x 22" strips in pairs. The units should measure 3½" wide when sewn. Press seams toward purple fabric. Layer strips with opposing seams and cut each strip into 10 segments, each 2" wide. Sew segments together, using ¼"-wide seam allowances, and press flat.

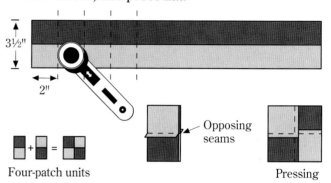

Four-patch units

Opposing seams

Pressing

2. Stitch 25 Milky Way blocks. Take care that fabrics match on adjoining blocks by placing fabrics in position on a design wall before stitching.

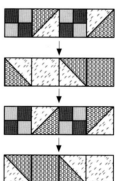

3. Stitch 5 rows of 5 blocks together. Join to form quilt top.
4. Stitch 5 side units, join together, and add to right side of quilt.
5. Stitch 5 bottom units. Add a corner unit on the right side and join to quilt top.

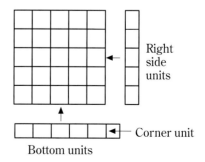

Right side units

Corner unit

Bottom units

6. Layer with batting and backing; quilt or tie. See page 138 for a quilting suggestion.

7. Bind with straight-grain or bias strips of fabric.

Milky Way *by Cleo Nollette, 1992, Seattle, Washington, 69" x 69". This lively scrap quilt is made from a classic collection of indigo-and-white prints, a traditional favorite. Quilted by Hazel Montague. (Collection of That Patchwork Place, Inc.)*

Mrs. Keller's Ninepatch

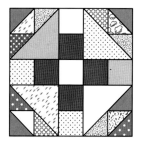

Mrs. Keller's Ninepatch
12½" block

Dimensions: 60" x 85"

24 blocks, 12½", set 4 across and 6 down; 5"-wide border.

Materials: 44"-wide fabric

2 yds. dark green print for blocks and border
1 strip, 3⅜" x 42", each of 14 different medium or dark prints, predominantly browns, greens, and golds for blocks (Nearest cut is ⅛ yd.)
1 strip, 10" x 42", each of 5 different light prints for blocks (Nearest cut is ⅓ yd.)
1 strip, 5⅞" x 42", each of 8 additional light prints for blocks (Nearest cut is ¼ yd.)
5⅛ yds. fabric for backing
⅝ yd. fabric for 308" of narrow binding
Batting and thread to finish

Cutting: All measurements include ¼" seams.

From the dark green print:
Cut 8 strips, 5½" x 42", for border.
Cut 8 strips, 3" x 42", for blocks.

From each of the 14 different medium or dark strips:
Cut 11 squares, 3⅜" x 3⅜", for a total of 154 squares. Cut once diagonally into 308 half-square triangles for blocks. You will have 20 triangles left over; save for another project.

From each of the 5 different light strips:
Cut 2 strips, 3" x 42", for a total of 10 strips for blocks.
Cut 1 strip, 3⅜" x 42", for a total of 5 strips. Cut the strips into a total of 48 squares, 3⅜" x 3⅜". Cut once diagonally into 96 half-square triangles for blocks.

From each of the 8 additional light strips:
Cut 6 squares, 5⅞" x 5⅞", for a total of 48

squares. Cut once diagonally into 96 half-square triangles for blocks.

DIRECTIONS

1. Join the 3⅜" light half-square triangles, the 3⅜" medium or dark half-square triangles, and the 5⅞" light half-square triangles to make 96 units as shown. Combine the fabrics at random.

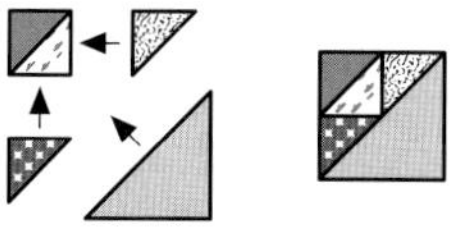

2. Join any 6 of the 3"-wide light print strips and 4 of the 3"-wide dark green strips to make 2 strip units as shown. The strip units should measure 13" wide when sewn. Cut the units into 24 segments, each 3" wide.

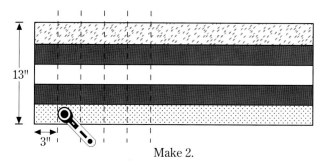

Make 2.

3. Join the remaining 3"-wide light print strips and 3"-wide dark green strips to make 4 strip units as shown. The strip units should measure 5½" wide when sewn. Cut the units into 48 segments, each 3" wide.

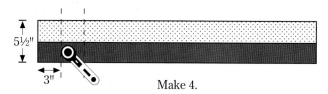

Make 4.

4. Join the pieces made in the previous steps to make 24 Mrs. Keller's Ninepatch blocks.

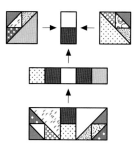

5. Set the blocks together in rows of 4 as shown in the quilt photo; join the rows.

6. Add dark green border, seaming strips as necessary. See "Borders with Straight-Cut Corners" on page 124.

7. Layer with batting and backing; quilt or tie. See page 138 for a quilting suggestion.

8. Bind with straight-grain or bias strips of fabric.

Not Quite Nine *by Julie Wilkinson Kimberlin, 1993, Anchorage, Alaska, 60″ x 85″. Julie captured the classic scrap-quilt look by using background fabrics that range from light to medium; the contrast varies from block to block. The small triangles feature a variety of interesting contemporary fabrics, including a rich brown-and-gold rooster print.*

Ocean Chain

Ocean Chain
Corner of quilt
(shown without borders)

Dimensions: 78" x 96"

Different units joined into diagonal bars; 6"-wide border.

Note: The antique quilt shown in the photo was made by attaching pieced lozenge-shaped units to plain squares, a method that requires numerous set-in corners. Our method—joining several different pieced units into diagonal bars—makes it easier to construct the quilt but results in a more random distribution of the fabrics in the "chains."

Materials: 44"-wide fabric

1 strip, 7" x 42", each of 24 different light and medium prints for "chains" (Nearest cut is ¼ yd.)*
1 strip, 7" x 42", each of 24 different dark prints for "chains" (Nearest cut is ¼ yd.)*
2⅞ yds. red-on-white or pink print for plain squares and border
5¾ yds. fabric for backing
¾ yd. fabric for 366" of narrow binding
Batting and thread to finish

*Use the same fabric more than once if you wish.

Cutting: All measurements include ¼" seams.

From each of the 7"-wide light and medium strips:
Cut 1 strip, 2⅝" x 42", for a total of 24 strips for "chains." Cut any 8 of these strips into a total of 112 squares, 2⅝" x 2⅝". Leave the remaining strips uncut.
Cut 2 squares, 4¼" x 4¼", for a total of 48 squares. Cut twice diagonally into 192 quarter-square triangles for "chains." You will have 4 triangles left over.

From each of the 7"-wide dark strips:
Cut 1 strip, 2⅝" x 42", for a total of 24 strips, for "chains." Cut any 8 of the strips into 112

squares, 2⅝" x 2⅝". Leave the remaining strips uncut.
Cut 2 squares, 4¼" x 4¼", for a total of 48 squares. Cut twice diagonally to make 192 quarter-square triangles for "chains." You will have 24 triangles left over.

From the red-on-white or pink print:
Cut 15 strips, 6½" x 42". Set aside 8 of the strips for seamed border. Cut the remaining 7 strips into 42 squares, 6½" x 6½".

DIRECTIONS

1. Using the light and dark quarter-square triangles and the light and dark 2⅝" squares, make Units AA, BB, and CC as shown. Combine the fabrics at random; use as many different combinations as possible.

Unit AA
Make 15.

Unit BB
Make 84.

Unit CC
Make 94.

2. Join 19 each of Units BB and CC to make 19 Unit DD as shown.

Unit DD
Make 19.

3. Join the uncut 2⅝" light and dark strips to make 8 strip units as shown. Combine the fabrics at random. The strip units should measure 9" wide when sewn. Cut the units into 120 segments, each 2⅝" wide. Join the segments to make 30 Unit A, using many combinations.

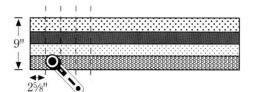

Unit A
Make 30.

4. Using the units you made in steps 1 and 2 and the 6½" red-on-white or pink print squares, make Units B, C, D, E, F, and G as shown.

Combine the "chain" fabrics at random.

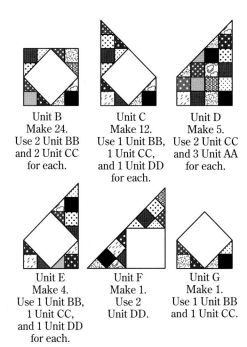

Unit B
Make 24.
Use 2 Unit BB
and 2 Unit CC
for each.

Unit C
Make 12.
Use 1 Unit BB,
1 Unit CC,
and 1 Unit DD
for each.

Unit D
Make 5.
Use 2 Unit CC
and 3 Unit AA
for each.

Unit E
Make 4.
Use 1 Unit BB,
1 Unit CC,
and 1 Unit DD
for each.

Unit F
Make 1.
Use 2
Unit DD.

Unit G
Make 1.
Use 1 Unit BB
and 1 Unit CC.

5. Set the units together in diagonal rows as shown; join the rows.

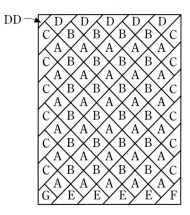

6. Add red-on-white borders, seaming strips as necessary. See "Borders with Straight-Cut Corners" on page 124.
7. Layer with batting and backing; quilt or tie. See page 138 for a quilting suggestion.
8. Bind with straight-grain or bias strips of fabric.

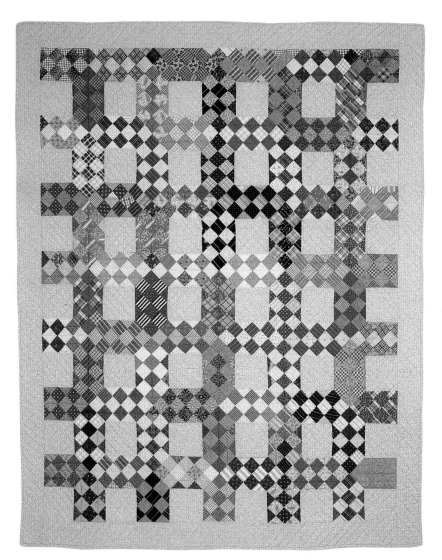

Ocean Chain *variation, maker unknown, c. 1920, Indiana, 67" x 85". The "waves" in this unique variation of the classic Ocean Waves design were made predominantly of squares instead of the more familiar triangles. Note: The pattern uses units sized more appropriately for rotary cutting and produces a 78" x 96" quilt. (Collection of Lucy J. Smith)*

Ohio Fence

Ohio Star
9" block

Rail Fence
9" block

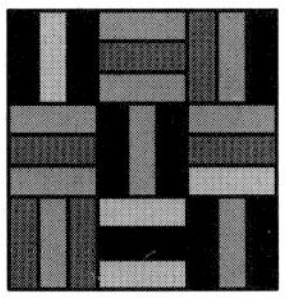

Dimensions: 63" x 81"

35 blocks (17 Ohio Star and 18 Rail Fence), 9", set 5 across and 7 down; 1½"-wide inner border, 7½"-wide outer border.

Note: The quilt pictured has 4 different light fabrics for the Ohio Star backgrounds and 2 different medium fabrics for a "collaged" outer border. The pattern provides for a single light fabric for the Ohio Star backgrounds and a single medium-colored fabric for the outer border.

Materials: 44"-wide fabric

1⅛ yds. dark green solid for blocks and inner border
½ yd. each of 3 additional dark green and blue-green solids for blocks
2¼ yds. medium green solid for blocks and outer border
½ yd. each of 3 additional medium green and blue-green solids for blocks
1 yd. light green or blue-green solid for blocks
3⅞ yds. fabric for backing
⅝ yd. fabric for 306" of narrow binding
Batting and thread to finish

Cutting: All measurements include ¼" seams.

From the 1⅛ yards of dark green solid:
Cut 8 strips, 2" x 42", for inner border.
Cut 1 strip, 4¼" x 42½"*. Cut the strip into 10 squares, 4¼" x 4¼". Cut twice diagonally into 40 quarter-square triangles for Ohio Star blocks.
Cut 2 strips, 3½" x 42". Cut the strips into a total of 17 squares, 3½" x 3½", for Ohio Star blocks.
Cut 4 strips, 1½" x 42", for Rail Fence blocks.

* If your strip does not measure 42½", you will need to cut the last square from leftovers.

From each of the 3 additional dark green and blue-green solids:
Cut 1 strip, 4¼" x 42", for a total of 3 strips. Cut the strips into 24 squares, 4¼" x 4¼". Cut twice diagonally into 96 quarter-square triangles for Ohio Star blocks.
Cut 7 strips, 1½" x 42", for a total of 21 strips for Rail Fence blocks.

From the 2¼ yards of medium green solid:
Cut 8 strips, 8" x 42", for outer border.
Cut 5 strips, 1½" x 42", for Rail Fence blocks.
Cut 5 squares, 4¼" x 4¼". Cut twice diagonally into 20 quarter-square triangles for Ohio Star blocks.

From each of the 3 additional medium green and blue-green solids:
Cut 6 strips, 1½" x 42", for a total of 18 strips for Rail Fence blocks.
Cut 4 squares, 4¼" x 4¼", for a total of 12 squares. Cut twice diagonally into 48 quarter-square triangles for Ohio Star blocks.

From the light green or blue-green solid:
Cut 7 strips, 3½" x 42". Cut the strips into a total of 68 squares, 3½" x 3½", for Ohio Star blocks.
Cut 2 strips, 4¼" x 42". Cut the strips into a total of 17 squares, 4¼" x 4¼". Cut twice diagonally into 68 quarter-square triangles for Ohio Star blocks.

DIRECTIONS

1. Using the quarter-square triangles and the light and dark squares, piece 17 Ohio Star blocks as shown. Combine the dark and medium fabrics at random.

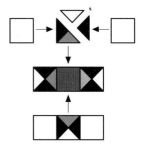

2. Join the 1½"-wide dark and medium strips to make 9 Strip Unit I and 7 Strip Unit II as shown. Combine the fabrics at random. The

strip units should measure 3½" wide when sewn. Cut the strip units into 3½"-wide segments. You will need 90 segments from Strip Units I and 72 segments from Strip Units II.

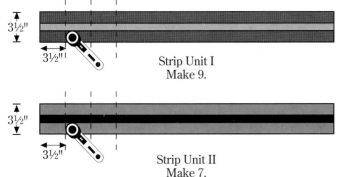

Strip Unit I
Make 9.

Strip Unit II
Make 7.

3. Join the segments into 18 Rail Fence blocks. Combine the segments at random.
4. Set the blocks together as shown in the quilt photo, alternating Rail Fence and Ohio Star blocks.
5. Add dark green inner border, seaming strips as necessary. See "Borders with Straight-Cut Corners" on page 124.
6. Add medium green outer border, as for inner border.
7. Layer with batting and backing; quilt or tie. See page 138 for a quilting suggestion.
8. Bind with straight-grain or bias strips of fabric.

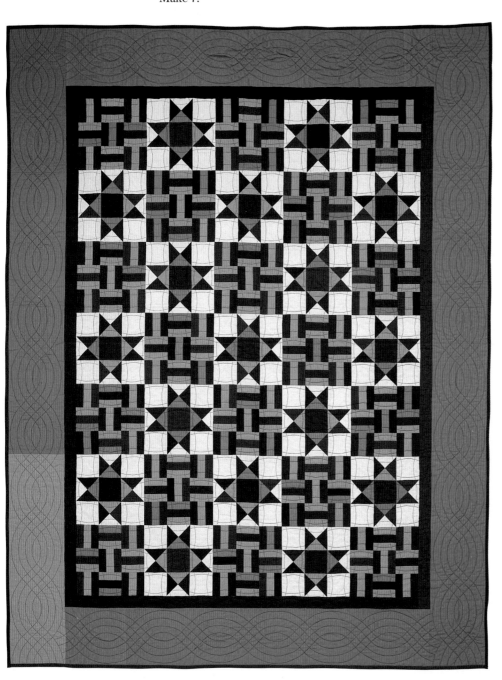

Ohio Fence *by George Taylor, 1993, Anchorage, Alaska, 63" x 81". George jazzed up this simple but striking design by using eleven different shades of green and blue-green arranged at random. The two-color outer border is a more obvious expression of his effective "mix and match" approach.*

Ohio Stars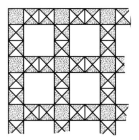

Ohio Stars
Corner of quilt

Dimensions: 66" x 84"

3" and 6" units joined in 2 different bar formats; finished without a border.

Materials: 44"-wide fabric

4⅔ yds. muslin for blocks
3½ yds. gold solid for blocks
5 yds. fabric for backing
⅝ yd. fabric for 318" of narrow binding
Batting and thread to finish

Cutting: All measurements include ¼" seams.

From the muslin:
   Cut 11 strips, 6½" x 42". Cut the strips into a total of 63 squares, 6½" x 6½".
   Cut 7 strips, 13½" x 42". Cut the strips into a total of 21 squares, 13½" x 13½", for bias strip piecing.

From the gold solid:
   Cut 8 strips, 3½" x 42". Cut the strips into a total of 80 squares, 3½" x 3½".
   Cut 7 strips, 13½" x 42". Cut the strips into a total of 21 squares, 13½" x 13½", for bias strip piecing.

DIRECTIONS

1. Place one of the 13½" muslin squares and one of the 13½" gold squares together right sides up to cut at the same time. Cut diagonally, corner to corner, to establish the bias, then cut bias strips 3½" wide. You will have 4 sets of strips plus 4 corner triangles. Set the corner triangles aside for another project.

13½" squares

2. Stitch bias strips together to make 2 strip-pieced units. Press all seams toward the gold fabric.

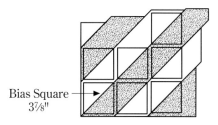

Bias Square
3⅞"

3. Using the Bias Square, cut 14 bias squares, each 3⅞" x 3⅞".
4. Match pairs of the 3⅞" bias squares, right sides together, nesting opposing seams. Make 14 Square Two units as shown on page 25.

Square Two

5. Repeat the above steps with the remaining 13½" squares. When you have cut and stitched all 42 squares, you will have a total of 294 Square Two units. You will have 10 left over; save for another project.
6. Join the Square Two units into 142 Square Two pairs as shown.

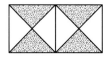

Square Two pairs

7. Combine 70 of the Square Two pairs with the 3½" gold squares to make 10 bars as shown. Each bar contains 7 Square Two pairs and 8 gold squares.

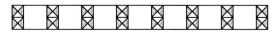

Make 10.

8. Combine the remaining Square Two pairs with the 6½" muslin squares to make 9 bars as shown. Each bar contains 8 Square Two pairs and 7 muslin squares.

Make 9.

9. Set the bars together as shown in the quilt
    photo, alternating the narrow and wide bars.
10. Layer with batting and backing; quilt or tie.

See page 139 for a quilting suggestion.
11. Bind with straight-grain or bias strips of fabric.

Ohio Star *bar quilt, maker and date unknown, purchased in Minnesota, 66" x 84".*
*The sashing forms the pattern in this crisp and sunny gold-and-muslin quilt. Like many
early quilts, this one is finished without a border. (Collection of Terri Shinn)*

Pinwheel Star

Pinwheel Star
16" block

Dimensions: 54" x 54"

9 blocks, 16", set as a bar quilt with 3 stars across and 3 down; 3"-wide border.

Materials: 44"-wide fabric

8 fat quarters of coordinating fabric for bias
    squares
½ yd. blue fabric for pinwheel
3 yds. star print for the setting pieces and border
3¼ yds. fabric for backing
½ yd. fabric for 220" of narrow binding
Batting and thread to finish

Cutting: All measurements include ¼" seams.

From each fat quarter of coordinating fabric:

Cut 14 squares, 2⅞" x 2⅞". Cut once diagonally into 28 triangles (224 total; you will use only 216). Pair the remainder of the fat quarters into sets of contrasting fabrics. Cut each pair of fabrics into 2½"-wide bias strips, following the directions for making bias squares on page 23. From this pieced fabric, cut 108 bias squares, 2½" x 2½".

From the blue fabric:

Cut 3 strips 4⅞" x 42". Cut the strips into a total of 18 squares, 4⅞" x 4⅞". Cut once diagonally into 36 triangles for pinwheels.

From the star print fabric:

Cut 4 lengthwise strips, 3¼" x 55", for border.
Cut 12 squares, 6⅛" x 6⅛", for Unit II.
Cut 4 squares, 4½" x 4½", for Unit III.
Cut 8 rectangles, 4½" x 8½", for Unit IV.
Cut 4 squares, 8½" x 8½", for Unit V.
Cut 3 squares, 9¼" x 9¼". Cut twice diagonally into 12 triangles for Unit VI.

DIRECTIONS

Note: To avoid seams through the large areas of background fabric, this quilt is constructed in units as a bar quilt. (See pages 123–24.)

Make all units and join completed units into rows. The stars and pinwheels will emerge after the quilt is set together. The units are identified below:

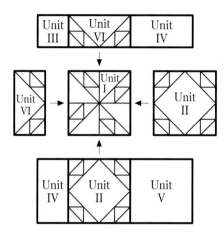

1. Piece 12 of Unit I, using large blue triangles, bias squares, and small triangles cut from coordinating fabric.

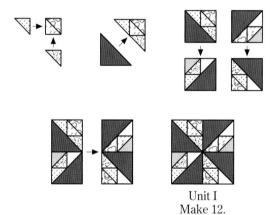

Unit I
Make 12.

2. Piece 12 of Unit II, using piecing diagram below as a guide.

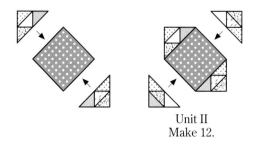

Unit II
Make 12.

Pinwheel Star *by Cleo Nollette, 1992, Seattle, Washington, 54" x 54". The stunning background and border fabric inspired this star quilt with a unique setting. This bar quilt was quilted in the ditch with occasional outline quilting to highlight the moon motifs. Quilted by Donna K. Gundlach. (Collection of Cleo Nollette)*

3. Piece 12 of Unit VI, using piecing diagram below as a guide.

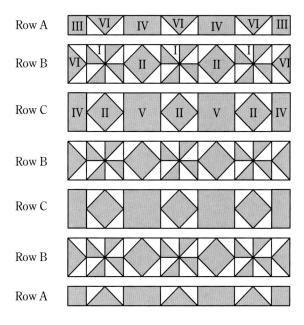

Unit 6
Make 12.

4. Join completed units to form rows. Join rows together as shown:

Row A

Row B

Row C

Row B

Row C

Row B

Row A

5. Add star print border, seaming strips as necessary. See "Borders with Mitered Corners" on page 125.
6. Layer with batting and backing; quilt or tie. See page 139 for a quilting suggestion.
7. Bind with straight-grain or bias strips of fabric.

Pot of Flowers

Pot of Flowers
12½" block

Dimensions: 65½" x 65½"

9 blocks, 12½", set on point with alternate unpieced blocks and set pieces; 1¾"-wide inner border and 4½"-wide outer border.

Materials: 44"-wide fabric

2 yds. pink-print background fabric
4 fat quarters of light pink for flowers
4 fat quarters of dark pink fabric for flowers
5 fat quarters of lavender fabric for pots
1 fat quarter of yellow print for flower centers
1 yd. green fabric for stems, leaves, and inner border
1¼ yds. pink fabric for pieced outer border
½ yd. fabric for 266" of narrow binding
4 yds. fabric for backing
Batting and thread to finish

Cutting: All measurements include ¼" seams.

Note: For Square Two units with the following coloration, you will have to make two different sets of bias squares, divide each in half, and then sew a segment from each set together.

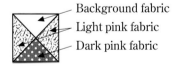

Background fabric
Light pink fabric
Dark pink fabric

From the pink-print background fabric:
Cut 4 pieces, 9" x 9".

From the light pink fat quarters:
Cut 8 pieces, 9" x 9". Pair 4 light pink pieces with 4 pink-print background pieces. Cut and piece 3"-wide bias strips, following the directions for making bias squares on page 23. From this pieced fabric, cut 27 bias squares, 3⅜" x 3⅜".

From the dark pink fat quarters:
Cut 4 pieces, 9" x 9". Pair each with a 9" x 9" piece of light pink. Cut and piece 3"-wide bias strips, following the directions for making bias squares on page 23. From this pieced fabric, cut 27 bias squares, 3⅜" x 3⅜". Pair bias squares of each coloration together and cut in half diagonally. Stitch together to make 54 Square Two units. (See pages 24–25.)

From the remaining pink-print background fabric:
Cut 4 squares, 13" x 13", for alternate blocks.
Cut 2 squares, 19" x 19". Cut twice diagonally into 8 side setting triangles.
Cut 2 squares, 9¾" x 9¾". Cut once diagonally into 4 corner setting pieces.
Cut 27 squares, 3" x 3", for blocks.
Cut 18 rectangles, 3" x 5½", for blocks.
Cut 5 squares, 6⅞" x 6⅞". Cut once diagonally into 10 triangles for blocks.
Cut 18 rectangles, 2" x 5", for blocks.
Cut 5 squares, 3⅞" x 3⅞". Cut once diagonally into 10 triangles for blocks.

From each lavender fat quarter:
Cut 1 square, 6⅞" x 6⅞". Cut once diagonally into 2 triangles (10 total) for pots.
Cut 1 square, 2⅜" x 2⅜". Cut once diagonally into 2 triangles (10 total) for base of pot.

From the yellow fat quarter:
Cut 27 squares, 3" x 3".

From the green fabric:
Cut 8 strips, 2¼" x 42", for inner border.
Cut remaining fabric into stems and leaves, following the appliqué directions on pages 29–30.

From the pink fabric for outer border:
Cut 8 strips, 4¾" x 42".

DIRECTIONS

1. Piece 9 Pot of Flowers blocks as shown. Use 2 matching Square Two units for each of the 3 flowers. Vary the flower colors in each pot.

Note: You will have one extra set of lavender pieces for the pot.

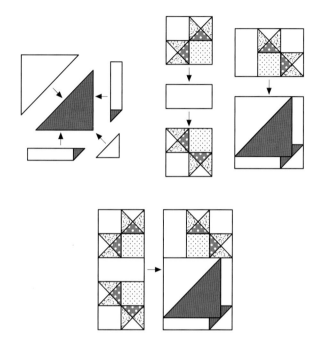

2. Appliqué 3 stems and 4 leaves to each block, following the directions on pages 29–30. Use bias strips and bias or Celtic bars to make the stems. Open previously sewn seams to insert the raw edges of the stem pieces. Resew these seams after appliqué is completed.

3. Stitch the completed blocks, the alternate blocks, and the setting pieces into diagonal rows. Stitch rows together.

4. Add green inner border, seaming strips as necessary. See "Borders with Straight-Cut Corners" on page 124.
5. Add pink outer border, seaming strips as necessary for borders with mitered corners (page 125).
6. Layer with batting and backing; quilt or tie. See page 139 for a quilting suggestion.
7. Bind with straight-grain or bias strips of fabric.

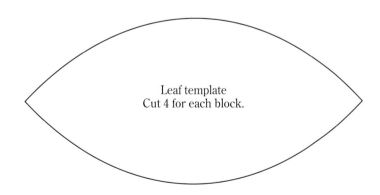

Leaf template
Cut 4 for each block.

Pot of Flowers *by Nancy J. Martin, 1992, Woodinville, Washington, 65½" x 65½". Square Two units comprise the lily-like flowers in this charming pastel quilt. Alternate blocks of background fabric feature feathered wreaths quilted by Alvina Nelson. The inner green border and appliqué leaves and stems offer an effective contrast to the other pastel fabrics. (Collection of That Patchwork Place, Inc.)*

Puss in a Corner

Puss in a Corner
7½" block

Dimensions: 89" x 96½"

110 blocks (55 Puss in a Corner and 55 alternate), 7½", set 10 across and 11 down; 7"-wide border.

Materials: 44"-wide fabric

2 yds. assorted light background fabrics for Puss in a Corner blocks
2 yds. total brown, tan, and navy blue fabrics
2½ yds. beige fabric for alternate blocks
2¼ yds. beige fabric for border
8 yds. coordinating fabric for backing
¾ yd. fabric for 380" of narrow binding
Batting and thread to finish

Cutting: All measurements include ¼" seams.

From the light background fabrics:
Cut 14 strips, 2¼" x 42".
Cut 7 strips, 4½" x 42".

From the brown, tan, and navy blue fabrics:
Cut 14 strips, 2¼" x 42".
Cut 7 strips, 4½" x 42".

From the beige fabric for alternate blocks:
Cut 11 strips, 8" x 42". Cut the strips into a total of 55 squares, 8" x 8".

From the beige fabric for border:
Cut 10 strips, 7¼" x 42".

DIRECTIONS

1. Join 2 of the 2¼" x 42" light background strips with 1 of the 4½" x 42" brown, tan, or navy blue strips; make 7 strip units as shown. The units should measure 8" wide when sewn. Cut the units into 55 segments, 4½" wide.

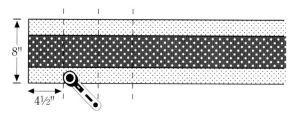

2. Join a 4½" x 42" light background strip and 2 of the 2¼" x 42" brown, tan, or navy blue strips; make 7 strip units as shown. The units should measure 8" wide when sewn. Cut the units into 110 segments, 2¼" wide.

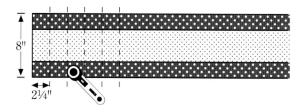

3. Join segments together to piece 55 Puss in a Corner blocks.

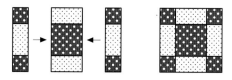

4. Join 5 Puss in a Corner blocks and 5 alternate blocks into a row. Make 11 rows.
5. Join rows for the quilt top as shown in quilt photo.
6. Add beige border, seaming strips as necessary. See "Borders with Straight-Cut Corners" on page 124.
7. Layer with batting and backing; quilt or tie. See page 139 for a quilting suggestion.
8. Bind with straight-grain or bias strips of fabric.

Puss in a Corner, *origin unknown, c. 1890, 89" x 96½". The soft browns, beiges, and indigos of this antique quilt create a tranquil composition, just right for a soothing bedcover. Lavish quilting by Hazel Montague contributes to the overall design. (Collection of That Patchwork Place, Inc.)*

The Railroad

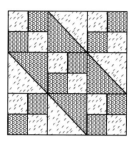

The Railroad
12" block

Dimensions: 72" x 84"

42 blocks (21 Railroad and 21 alternate), 12", set 6 across and 7 down; finished without a border.

Materials: 44"-wide fabric

1 strip, 5" x 42", each of 21 different light prints for Railroad blocks* (Nearest cut is ¼ yd.)
1 strip, 5" x 42", each of 21 different dark prints, predominantly brown and black with some red, some navy blue for Railroad blocks* (Nearest cut is ¼ yd.)
2½ yds. red print for alternate blocks
5 yds. fabric for backing
¾ yd. fabric for 330" of narrow binding
Batting and thread to finish

* Use the same fabric more than once if you wish.

Cutting: All measurements include ¼" seams.

From each of the light and dark strips:
Cut 2 squares, 4⅞" x 4⅞", for a total of 42 light and 42 dark squares. Cut once diagonally into 84 light and 84 dark half-square triangles for Railroad blocks.
Cut 1 strip, 2½" x approximately 27", for a total of 42 strips for Railroad blocks.

From the red print:
Cut 7 strips, 12½" x 42". Cut the strips into a total of 21 squares, 12½" x 12½", for alternate blocks.

DIRECTIONS

1. Join one of the 2½"-wide light strips and one of the 2½"-wide dark strips to make a strip unit as shown. Pick a fabric combination that you find pleasing. The strip unit should measure 4½" wide when sewn. Cut the strip unit into 10 segments, each 2½" wide. Join the segments to make 5 Four Patch units as shown.

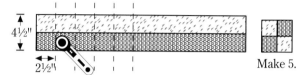

Make 5.

2. Using the same fabric combination as in step 1, join 4 light half-square triangles and 4 dark half-square triangles to make 4 half-square triangle units as shown.

Make 4.

3. Join the Four Patch units and the half-square triangle units to make a Railroad block as shown.

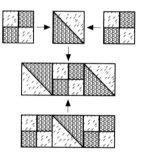

4. Repeat steps 1-3 with the remaining light and dark strips and half-square triangles. You will have a total of 21 Railroad blocks.
5. Set the Railroad blocks together with the 12½" red squares as shown in the quilt photo, alternating Railroad blocks and red squares.
6. Layer with batting and backing; quilt or tie. See page 139 for a quilting suggestion.
7. Bind with straight-grain or bias strips of fabric.

The Railroad, *origin unknown, c. 1900, 72" x 84". Purchased as a top in Anchorage, Alaska, and quilted in 1993 by Debby Coates, this graphic classic quilt sports an interesting assortment of subdued turn-of-the-century prints, enlivened by the cheery red alternate blocks. (Collection of Debby Coates)*

Scot's Plaid

Scot's Plaid
10" block

Dimensions: 62½" x 82½"

48 blocks, 10", set 6 across and 8 down with 2½"-wide sashing on left and bottom edges; finished without a border.

Materials: 44"-wide fabric

½ yd. dark green print for blocks
¼ yd. each of 6 different dark green and blue-green prints for blocks
1 strip, 5½" x 42", each of 8 different light and medium gold and tan prints for blocks (Nearest cut is ¼ yd.)
2⅛ yds. medium brown print for blocks and sashing
3⅞ yds. fabric for backing
⅝ yd. fabric for 308" of narrow binding
Batting and thread to finish

Cutting: All measurements include ¼" seams.

From the ½ yard of dark green print:
Cut 1 strip, 5½" x 42". Cut the strip into 6 squares, 5½" x 5½", for blocks.
Cut 3 strips, 3" x 42", for blocks.
Cut 1 square, 3" x 3", for sashing.

From each of the 6 dark green and blue-green prints:
Cut 1 strip, 5½" x 42", for a total of 6 strips. Cut these strips into a total of 42 squares, 5½" x 5½", for blocks. You will have a total of 48 squares, including the 5½" dark green squares you cut earlier.
Cut 1 strip, 3" x 42", for blocks. You will have a total of 9 strips, including the 3"-wide dark green strips you cut earlier.

From the light and medium gold and tan strips:
Cut any 4 of the strips into 3"-wide segments, to make 48 rectangles, 3" x 5½", for blocks. Leave the remaining 4 strips uncut.

From the medium brown print:
Cut 9 strips, 8" x 42", for blocks and sashing. Cut 4 of the strips into 3"-wide segments, to make 48 rectangles, 3" x 8". Leave the remaining 5 strips uncut.

DIRECTIONS

1. Join the 3" x 5½" light and medium gold and tan rectangles to the 5½" dark green and blue-green squares to make 48 units as shown. Combine the fabrics at random.

2. Join any 4 of the 3"-wide dark green and blue-green strips to the 4 uncut 5½"-wide light and medium gold and tan strips to make 4 strip units as shown. The strip units should measure 8" wide when sewn. Cut the units into 48 segments, each 3" wide.

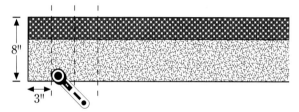

3. Join the segments you cut in the previous step to the units you made in step 1 to make 24 each of the units shown below. Combine the fabrics at random.

Make 24.   Make 24.

4. Join the 3" x 8" medium brown rectangles to the units you made in the previous step to make 48 units as shown, rotating the units you made in the previous step as needed.

Make 48.

5. Join the remaining 3"-wide dark green and blue-green strips to the uncut 8" medium brown strips to make 5 strip units as shown. The strip units should measure 10½" wide when sewn. Cut the units into 62 segments, each 3" wide.

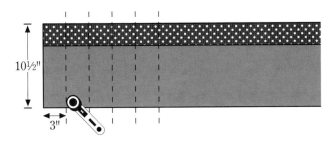

6. Join 48 of the segments you cut in the previous step to the units you made in step 3 to make 48 Scot's Plaid blocks.
7. Set the blocks together in rows of 6 as shown

in the quilt photo, adding one of the segments from step 4 to the left side of each row. Join the rows.
8. Join the remaining segments from step 4 and the 3" dark green square to make a sashing strip to add to the bottom of the quilt as shown.

9. Layer with batting and backing; quilt or tie. See page 140 for a quilting suggestion.
10. Bind with straight-grain or bias strips of fabric.

John Doe *by Dee Morrow, 1993, Anchorage, Alaska, 62½" x 82½". Challenged to make a quilt that would appeal to men and boys, Dee used the traditional Scot's Plaid pattern and an eclectic selection of green, blue, and brown prints. Perle-cotton quilting echoes the pieced plaid design.*

Shoo Fly Star

Shoo Fly
8" block

Sawtooth Star
8" block

Dimensions: 66" x 82"

63 blocks (32 Shoo Fly and 31 Sawtooth Star), 8",
set 7 across and 9 down; 5"-wide border.

Materials: 44"-wide fabric

2½ yds. assorted light and dark red plaids, stripes,
  checks, and small prints
2 yds. assorted light and dark blue plaids, stripes,
  checks, and small prints
1 yd. assorted large-scale prints or chintzes with
  light background for Shoo Fly centers
1 yd. assorted red or blue large-scale prints or
  chintzes for Sawtooth Star centers
1¼ yds. navy blue print for border
3¾ yds. fabric for backing
⅝ yd. fabric for 304" of narrow binding
Batting and thread to finish

Cutting: All measurements include ¼" seams.

**From the assorted red plaids, stripes, checks, and
small prints:**

Cut 12 light and 12 dark squares, each 7" x 7".
Pair a light and a dark square, then cut and piece
2½"-wide bias strips, following the directions for
making bias squares on page 23. From this pieced
fabric, cut 96 bias squares, 2½" x 2½". You need 4
matching bias squares for each red Shoo Fly block.

**From the assorted blue plaids, stripes, checks, and
small prints:**

Cut 4 light and 4 dark squares, each 7" x 7".
Pair a light and a dark square, then cut and piece
2½"-wide bias strips, following the directions for
making bias squares on page 23. From this pieced
fabric, cut 32 bias squares, 2½" x 2½". You need 4
matching bias squares for each blue Shoo Fly block.

**From the assorted large-scale prints or chintzes with
light background:**

Cut 32 squares, 4½" x 4½", for the Shoo Fly
block centers.

**From the assorted red and blue large-scale prints or
chintzes:**

Cut 31 squares, 4½" x 4½", for the Sawtooth
Star centers.

**From the remaining red plaids, stripes, checks, and
small prints:**

Cut 96 rectangles, 2½" x 4½", for Shoo Fly
blocks.
Cut 84 squares, 2⅞" x 2⅞". Cut once diago-
nally into 168 triangles for Sawtooth Star tips.
Cut 21 squares, 5¼" x 5¼". Cut twice diago-
nally into 84 triangles for Sawtooth Star blocks.
Cut 84 squares, 2½" x 2½", for corners of
Sawtooth Star blocks.

**From the remaining blue plaids, stripes, checks,
and small prints:**

Cut 32 rectangles, 2½" x 4½", for Shoo Fly
blocks.
Cut 20 squares, 2⅞" x 2⅞". Cut once diago-
nally into 40 triangles for Sawtooth Star tips.
Cut 10 squares, 5¼" x 5¼". Cut twice diago-
nally into 40 triangles for Sawtooth Star blocks.
Cut 40 squares, 2½" x 2½", for corners of
Sawtooth Star blocks.

From the navy blue print for border:
Cut 8 strips, 5¼" x 42".

DIRECTIONS

1. Piece 24 red Shoo Fly blocks
    and 8 blue Shoo Fly blocks,
    using the light background
    chintz squares in the center.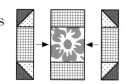

2. Piece 21 red Sawtooth Star
    blocks and 10 blue Sawtooth
    Star blocks, using the red or
    blue large-scale prints or
    chintzes in the center.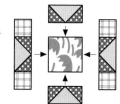

3. Join together in rows of 7 blocks, alternating
    the Shoo Fly and Sawtooth Star blocks. Ar-
    range colors as shown in the quilt photo. Join
    rows together, beginning and ending with a
    row that has the Shoo Fly block in the corner.

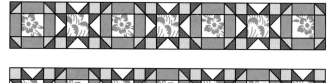

4. Add navy blue border, seaming strips as necessary. See "Borders with Straight-Cut Corners" on page 124 .

5. Layer with batting and backing; quilt or tie. See page 140 for a quilting suggestion.
6. Bind with straight-grain or bias strips of fabric.

Shoo Fly Star *by Mariet Soethout, 1988, Amsterdam, Netherlands, 66″ x 82″. Traditional costume fabrics used in the various Netherlands' villages were used in this two-block quilt. Mariet based her design on* A Dozen Variables *by Nancy J. Martin and Marsha McCloskey, That Patchwork Place, Inc., 1988. (Photo courtesy of* den haan *and* wagenmakers.*)*

Snowbows

Four Patch
6" block

Snowball
6" block

Dimensions: 71" x 83"

99 blocks (49 Four Patch and 50 Snowball), 6", set 9 across and 11 down with half and quarter blocks to complete the outside edges; 5½"-wide border.

Materials: 44"-wide fabric

3½ yds. red print for blocks and border
1½ yds. tan print for blocks
1½ yds. gray print for blocks
5 yds. fabric for backing
¾ yd. fabric for 326" of narrow binding
Batting and thread to finish

Cutting: All measurements include ¼" seams.

From the red print:
Cut 8 strips, 6" x 42", for border.
Cut 11 strips, 6½" x 42". Cut 9 of the strips into a total of 50 squares, 6½" x 6½", for Snowball blocks. Cut the remaining 2 strips into a total of 18 segments, each 3½" wide, to make rectangles 3½" x 6½" for half blocks.
Cut 4 squares, 3½" x 3½", for quarter blocks.

From the tan print:
Cut 11 strips, 3½" x 42", for Four Patch blocks.
Cut 4 strips, 2⅜" x 42". Cut the strips into a total of 60 squares, 2⅜" x 2⅜". Cut once diagonally into 120 half-square triangles for Snowball blocks.

From the gray print:
Cut 11 strips, 3½" x 42", for Four Patch blocks.
Cut 4 strips, 2⅜" x 42". Cut the strips into a total of 60 squares, 2⅜" x 2⅜". Cut once diagonally into 120 half-square triangles for Snowball blocks.

DIRECTIONS

1. Using the trimming template on page 143, trim all 4 corners from each 6½" red square. (See "Trimming Templates" on page 22.) Trim 2 corners from each 3½" x 6½" red rectangle and 1 corner from each 3½" red square as shown.

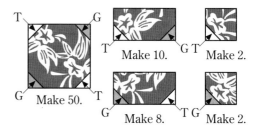

2. Join tan and gray half-square triangles to the trimmed corners of the large and small squares and the rectangles as shown. Follow the color-placement notes on the diagrams carefully: T = Tan; G = Gray.

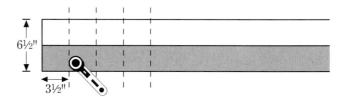

Make 50. Make 10. Make 2. Make 8. Make 2.

3. Join the 3½"-wide tan and gray strips to make 11 strip units as shown. The strip units should measure 6½" wide when sewn. Cut the units into 120 segments, each 3½" wide.

4. Join 98 of the 3½"-wide segments to make 49 Four Patch blocks. The remaining 22 segments are half blocks.

5. Set the Four Patch blocks and the Snowball blocks together as shown in the quilt photo, alternating the blocks. Tan half-square triangles must be adjacent to tan squares, and gray half-square triangles adjacent to gray squares, to form the pattern of tan and gray bow ties. Note that the half and quarter blocks are joined to the outside edges of the quilt to complete the Bow Tie pattern.

6. Add red print border, seaming strips as necessary. See "Borders with Straight-Cut Corners" on page 124.

7. Layer with batting and backing; quilt or tie. See page 140 for a quilting suggestion.

8. Bind with straight-grain or bias strips of fabric.

Snowbows *by Judy Hopkins, 1993, Anchorage, Alaska, 71″ x 83″. Judy suffered severe "Bow Tie burnout" after she finished her 1990 book,* Fit To Be Tied, *but when she realized that Four Patch and Snowball blocks combine nicely to make Bow Ties, she couldn't resist doing it "just one more time!" Quilted by Julie Kimberlin. (Collection of Julie Wilkinson Kimberlin)*

Split Rail Fence

Block A
10" block

Block B
10" block

Dimensions: 56" x 76"

35 blocks (18 Block A and 17 Block B), 10", set 5 across and 7 down; 3"-wide border.

Materials: 44"-wide fabric

¼ yd. each of 6 different dark blue prints for blocks
¼ yd. each of 4 different light prints for blocks
¾ yd. Stripe A for Block A
1 yd. Stripe B for Block B
⅞ yd. Stripe C for border
3½ yds. fabric for backing
⅝ yd. fabric for 282" of narrow binding
Batting and thread to finish

Cutting: All measurements include ¼" seams.

From each of the dark blue prints and the light prints:
Cut 3 strips, 2½" x 42", for a total of 18 dark blue strips and 12 light strips for blocks.

From Stripe A:
Cut 9 strips, 2½" x 42". Cut the strips into a total of 36 segments, each 10½" wide, to make rectangles, 2½" x 10½", for Block A.

From Stripe B:
Cut 13 strips, 2½" x 42". Cut the strips into a total of 51 segments, each 10½" wide, to make rectangles, 2½" x 10½", for Block B.

From Stripe C:
Cut 8 strips, 3½" x 42", for border.

DIRECTIONS

1. Join the 2½"-wide dark blue and light strips to make 6 strip units as shown. Combine the fabrics at random. The strip units should measure 10½" wide when sewn. Cut the units into a total of 88 segments, each 2½" wide.

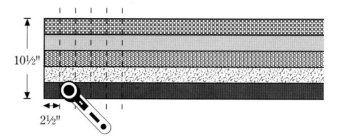

2. Join 54 of the 2½"-wide segments with the Stripe A rectangles to make 18 Block A.

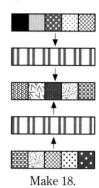

Make 18.

3. Join the remaining 2½"-wide segments with the Stripe B rectangles to make 17 Block B.

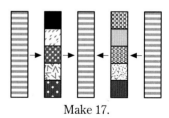

Make 17.

4. Set the blocks together in rows of 5 as shown in the quilt photo, alternating Block A and Block B; join the rows.
5. Add stripe C border, seaming strips as necessary. See "Borders with Straight-Cut Corners" on page 124.
6. Layer with batting and backing; quilt or tie. See page 140 for a quilting suggestion.
7. Bind with straight-grain or bias strips of fabric.

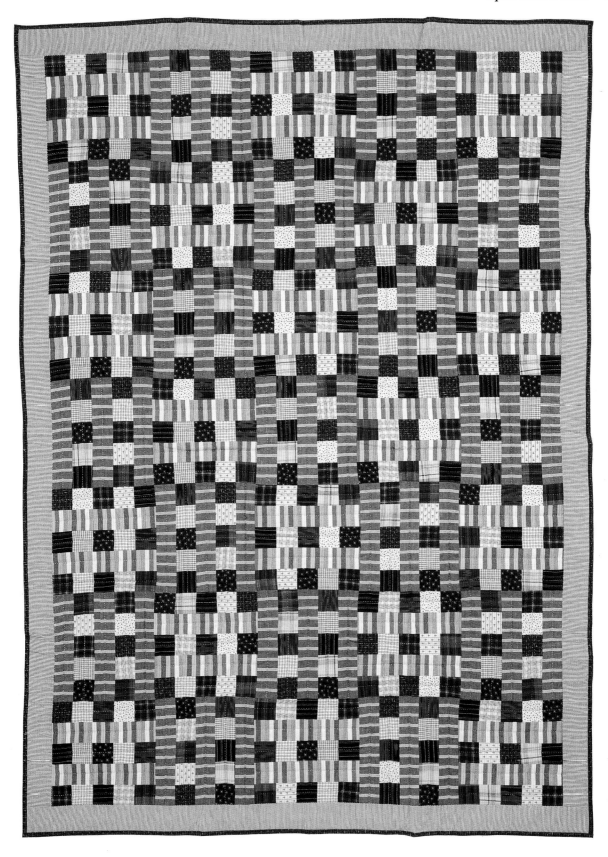

Split Rail Fence *by Judy Hopkins, 1992, Anchorage, Alaska, 56" x 76". Judy got carried away with striped chambrays! The antique quilt that inspired her was done in slightly more subdued solids—red and white squares set against mint green strips. This easy quilt would be effective in a number of fabric and color combinations. (Collection of Darien and Jeff Reece)*

Square on Square

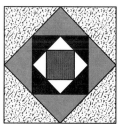

Square on Square
9" block

Dimensions: 75" x 89"

20 blocks, 9", set 4 across and 5 down with 3"-wide strip-pieced sashing strips and Pinwheel sashing squares; 6"-wide inner border, 9"-wide outer border.

Materials: 44"-wide fabric

1⅛ yds. blue print for blocks and sashing squares

1½ yds. medium blue-gray solid for blocks and sashing

2⅛ yds. light blue solid for sashing, sashing squares, and inner border

2½ yds. blue-green solid for outer border

4" x 26" rectangles of 7 different light, medium, and dark blue solids for blocks* (Nearest cut is ⅛ yd.)

5⅜ yds. fabric for backing

¾ yd. fabric for 346" of narrow binding

Batting and thread to finish

* Try 1 light, 3 mediums, and 3 darks.

Cutting: All measurements include ¼" seams.

From the blue print:

Cut 6 strips, 5⅜" x 42". Cut the strips into a total of 40 squares, 5⅜" x 5⅜". Cut once diagonally into 80 half-square triangles for blocks (A).

Cut 2 strips, 2⅜" x 42". Cut the strips into a total of 24 squares, 2⅜" x 2⅜". Cut once diagonally into 48 half-square triangles for sashing squares.

From the medium blue-gray solid:

Cut 4 strips, 5¾" x 42". Cut the strips into a total of 20 squares, 5¾" x 5¾". Cut twice diagonally to make 80 quarter-square triangles for blocks (B).

Cut 18 strips, 1½" x 42", for sashing. Cut 2 of these strips into 8 segments, each 9½" wide, to make rectangles, 1½" x 9½". Leave the remaining 16 strips uncut.

From the light blue solid:

Cut 8 strips, 6½" x 42", for inner border.

Cut 2 strips, 2⅜" x 42". Cut these strips into 24 squares, 2⅜" x 2⅜". Cut once diagonally into 48 half-square triangles for sashing squares.

Cut 8 strips, 1½" x 42", for sashing.

Cut 1 rectangle, 4" x 26". Set aside with the other 4" x 26" rectangles.

From the blue-green solid:

Cut 8 strips, 9½" x 42", for outer border.

Cut 2 rectangles, 4" x 26". Set aside with the other 4" x 26" rectangles.

From each of the 4" x 26" pieces of assorted blue solids (10 total):

Cut 4 squares, 3⅛" x 3⅛", for a total of 40 squares. Cut once diagonally into 80 half-square triangles for blocks (C).

Cut 2 squares, 3½" x 3½", for a total of 20 squares. Cut twice diagonally into 80 quarter-square triangles for blocks (D).

Cut 2 squares, 2¾" x 2¾", for a total of 20 squares (E).

DIRECTIONS

1. Using pieces A, B, C, D, and E, piece 20 Square on Square blocks as shown. Note in the quilt photo that the blue print triangles (A) and the medium blue-gray triangles (B) appear in the same position in every block, but each block uses a different combination of fabrics for pieces C, D, and E.

2. *Optional:* Note in the quilt photo that the 4 blocks along the top edge of the quilt and the 4 blocks along the bottom edge of the quilt have extra medium blue-gray strips along their outside edges. You can either include or eliminate these strips. If you wish to include them, join a 1½" x 9½" medium blue-gray rectangle to one side of each of 8 of the Square on Square blocks.

3. Using the 2⅜" blue print and light blue solid half-square triangles, piece 12 Pinwheel blocks as shown.

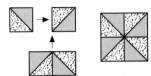

4. Join the 1½"-wide medium blue-gray and light blue strips to make 8 strip units as shown. The strip units should measure 3½" wide when sewn. From the strip units, cut a total of 25 segments, each 9½" wide, for sashing. If you have opted to include the extra strips on the top and bottom blocks, cut 6 sashing segments, each 10½" wide, to use in the top and

bottom rows. Otherwise, cut 6 more segments, each 9½" wide.

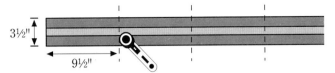

5. Set the blocks together with the sashing strips and the Pinwheel sashing squares as shown in the quilt photo.

6. Add light blue inner border, seaming strips as necessary. See "Borders with Straight-Cut Corners" on page 124.

7. Add blue-green outer border, as for inner border.

8. Layer with batting and backing; quilt or tie. See page 140 for a quilting suggestion.

9. Bind with straight-grain or bias strips of fabric.

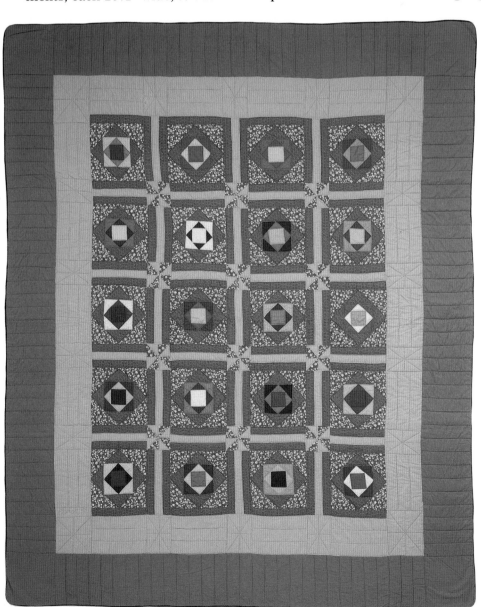

Just Blues Scrap
by Elinor Czarnecki, 1987, Cudahy, Wisconsin, 75" x 89". Inspired by a photo in a 1981 Country Living *magazine, Elinor made this quilt from scraps of two 4' x 15' wall hangings commissioned for a church. The subtle Pinwheel sashing squares add a fresh twist.*

Squares and Strips

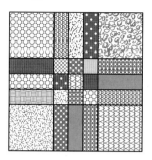

Squares and Strips
13½" block

Dimensions: 62½" x 79"

12 blocks, 13½", set 3 across and 4 down with 3"-wide sashing strips and corner squares; 5"-wide border.

Materials: 44"-wide fabric

⅓ yd. each of 3 different bright prints in warm colors (red, red-orange, orange, red-violet, hot pink), for blocks

¼ yd. each of 5 additonal bright prints in warm colors for blocks

⅛ yd. each of 8 different bright prints in cool colors (green, blue-green, blue, blue-violet, purple) for blocks

1¼ yds. bright turquoise print for sashing strips

¼ yd. bright red print for sashing squares

1⅓ yds. bright multicolored print for border

3⅞ yds. fabric for backing

⅝ yd. fabric for 301" of narrow binding

Batting and thread to finish

Cutting: All measurements include ¼" seams.

From each of the 3 bright prints in warm colors (the ⅓-yard pieces):
Cut 1 strip, 5" x 42", for a total of 3 strips. Cut these strips into a total of 18 squares, 5" x 5", for blocks.
Cut 2 strips, 2" x 42", for a total of 6 strips for blocks.

From each of the 5 additional bright prints in warm colors (the ¼-yard pieces):
Cut 1 strip, 5" x 42" for a total of 5 strips. Cut these strips into a total of 30 squares, 5" x 5", for blocks. You will have a total of 48 warm squares, including those you cut above.
Cut 1 strip, 2" x 42", for a total of 5 strips for blocks. You will have a total of 11 warm color strips, including those you cut above.

From each of the 8 bright prints in cool colors:
Cut 2 strips, 2" x 42", for a total of 16 strips for blocks.

From the turquoise print:
Cut 3 strips, 14" x 42". Cut these strips into segments, each 3½" wide, to make 31 rectangles, 3½" x 14", for sashing strips.

From the red print:
Cut 2 strips, 3½" x 42". Cut these strips into a total of 20 squares, 3½" x 3½", for sashing squares.

From the multicolored print:
Cut 8 strips, 5½" x 42", for border.

DIRECTIONS

1. Join any 4 of the 2"-wide warm strips and any 2 of the 2"-wide cool strips to make 2 strip units as shown. The strip units should measure 5" wide when sewn. Cut the units into 24 segments, each 2" wide.

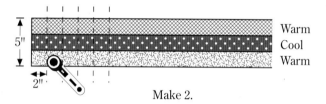

Make 2.

2. Join the remaining 2"-wide warm and cool strips to make 7 strip units as shown. The strip units should measure 5" wide when sewn. Cut 1 of the strip units into 12 segments, each 2" wide. Cut the remaining 6 strip units into a total of 48 segments, each 5" wide.

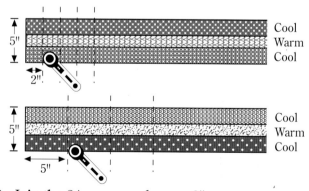

3. Join the 24 warm-cool-warm 2"-wide segments and the 12 cool-warm-cool 2"-wide segments to make 12 Ninepatch units with warm corners as shown.

4. Join the Ninepatch units, the 5" warm squares, and the 5"-wide cool-warm-cool segments to make 12 Squares and Strips blocks.

5. Set the blocks together with the sashing strips and sashing squares as shown in the quilt photo. (See "Straight Sets" on page 120.)

6. Add multicolored print border, seaming strips as necessary. See "Borders with Straight-Cut Corners" on page 124.

7. Layer with batting and backing; quilt or tie. See page 140 for a quilting suggestion.

8. Bind with straight-grain or bias strips of fabric.

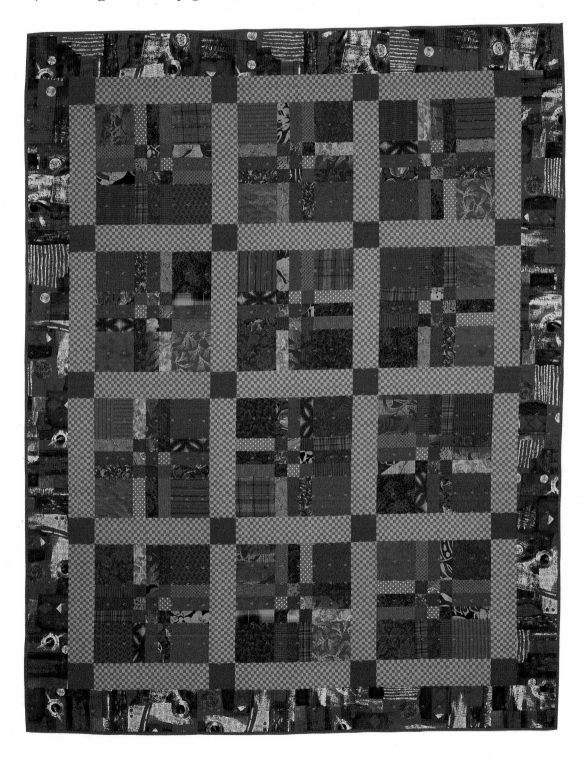

Jujubes *by Judy Hopkins, 1992, Anchorage, Alaska, 62½" x 79". Judy updated an unnamed traditional block by using bright, contemporary jewel-toned prints. Quilted by Sarah Kaufman. (Collection of Sarah Pasma Kaufman)*

Stars in the Sashing

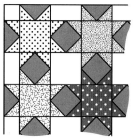

Stars in the Sashing
Corner of quilt

Dimensions: 68" x 85"

Different pieced and plain units joined in 3 different bar formats; finished without a border.

Note: We have simplified the cutting and piecing of this quilt by substituting Sawtooth Stars for the eight-pointed stars used in the original quilt. The overall appearance of the quilt made from this pattern will be very similar to that of the pictured quilt.

Materials: 44"-wide fabric

1 piece, 6½" x 12", each of 80 different prints for stars*
1½ yds. yellow solid for background
1⅝ yds. purple solid for background
5⅛ yds. fabric for backing
¾ yd. fabric for 324" of narrow binding
Batting and thread to finish

* Use a fabric more than once if you wish. If purchasing fabric, ⅜ yd. each of 14 different prints will yield 84 pieces, 6½" x 12".

Cutting: All measurements include ¼" seams.

From each of the 80 different prints:
Cut 1 square, 4¾" x 4¾", for star center.
Cut 4 squares, 3" x 3". Cut once diagonally into 8 half-square triangles for star points.

From the yellow solid:
Cut 10 strips, 4¾" x 42". Cut 8 of the strips into a total of 63 squares, 4¾" x 4¾". Cut the remaining 2 strips into 2⅝"-wide segments, to make 32 rectangles, 2⅝" x 4¾", for background.
Cut 4 squares, 2⅝" x 2⅝", for corners.

From the purple solid:
Cut 13 strips, 3½" x 42". Cut the strips into a total of 142 squares, 3½" x 3½", for background.
Cut 2 strips, 5½" x 42". Cut the strips into a total of 9 squares, 5½" x 5½". Cut twice diagonally into 36 quarter-square triangles for background.

DIRECTIONS

Important: Three different bar formats combine to form the overall pattern of this quilt. To ensure that the star points will be the same fabric as the star centers throughout the quilt, lay out the pieces for several bars—or for the entire quilt—before you start to sew!

1. Join 3" print half-square triangles to the 3½" purple squares to make 142 Unit I. Join the remaining 3" print half-square triangles to the 5½" purple quarter-square triangles to make 36 Unit II as shown. Arrange the printed fabrics so that complete, single-fabric stars will form when the quilt is assembled as noted above.

Unit I   Unit II

2. Join the units and the yellow squares and rectangles to make 1 top bar, 1 bottom bar, 10 Bar A, and 9 Bar B as shown. The top and bottom bars include the 2⅝" yellow squares. Lay out several bars, matching the prints in the star points with the prints in the star centers, before you sew.

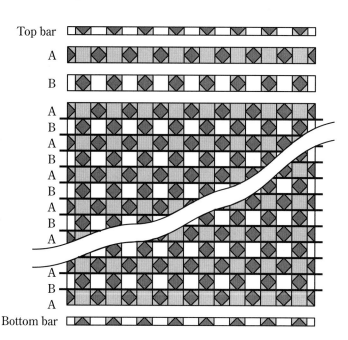

3. Join the bars.
4. If desired, trim the corners of the quilt at a 45° angle as shown in the quilt photo.

5. Layer with batting and backing; quilt or tie. See page 141 for a quilting suggestion.
6. Bind with straight-grain or bias strips of fabric.

Stars of Youth *by Lavonne DeBoer, 1937, Harrison, South Dakota, 80″ x 98″. This is a true scrap quilt. Lavonne made the stars from scraps of clothing before she was eighteen years old; after she married, her mother-in-law helped her complete the quilt. Quilted by Nellie and Lavonne DeBoer. Note: The pattern substitutes easier-to-make Sawtooth Stars for Lavonne's eight-pointed stars and produces a 68″ x 85″ quilt.*

Stars in Strips

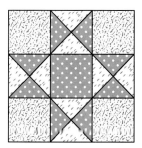

Ohio Star
10½" block

Dimensions: 77" x 89"*

18 Ohio Star blocks, 10½", set on point in 3 strips of 6 stars each; star strips separated by 8"-wide vertical bars; finished without a border.

*Finished size will vary with size of setting triangles and trimming.

Materials: 44"-wide fabric

1⅝ yds. light background print for stars
1 yd. light-medium background print for star corners
1 yd. medium blue print for stars
⅞ yd. medium gray print for stars
½ yd. tan print for stars
2⅝ yds. light gray print for setting triangles
2⅝ yds. gray "chintz" print for bars
5⅜ yds. fabric for backing
¾ yd. fabric for 350" of narrow binding
Batting and thread to finish

Cutting: All measurements include ¼" seams.

From the light background print:
Cut 4 strips, 13½" x 42". Cut these strips into a total of 12 squares, 13½" x 13½", for bias strip piecing.

From the light-medium background print:
Cut 8 strips, 4" x 42". Cut these strips into a total of 72 squares, 4" x 4", for star corners.

From the medium blue print:
Cut 1 strip, 4" x 42". Cut this strip into 9 squares, 4" x 4", for star centers.
Cut 2 strips, 13½" x 42". Cut these strips into 6 squares, 13½" x 13½", for bias strip piecing.

From the medium gray print:
Cut 6 squares, 4" x 4", for star centers.
Cut 4 squares, 13½" x 13½", for bias strip piecing.

From the tan print:
Cut 3 squares, 4" x 4", for star centers.
Cut 2 squares, 13½" x 13½", for bias strip piecing.

From the light gray print:
Cut 8 squares, 16¼" x 16¼". Cut twice diagonally into 32 quarter-square triangles for side setting triangles. You will have 2 triangles left over.
Cut 2 strips, 13" x 42". Cut these strips into 6 squares, 13" x 13". Cut diagonally into 12 half-square triangles for corner setting triangles.

From the gray "chintz" print:
Cut 4 lengthwise strips, 8½" x at least 92", for bars.

DIRECTIONS

1. Place one of the 13½" light background print squares and one of the 13½" medium blue squares together right sides up to cut at the same time. Cut diagonally, corner to corner, to establish the bias, then cut bias strips 3⅞" wide. You will have 2 sets of strips plus 4 corner triangles.

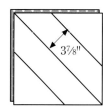

13½" squares

2. Stitch bias strips together to make 2 pieces of stripped fabric. Press all seams toward the darker fabric.

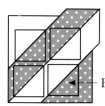

Bias square
4⅜"

3. Using the Bias Square, cut 4 bias squares, each 4⅜" x 4⅜".
4. Match pairs of the 4⅜" bias squares, right sides together, nesting opposing seams. Make 4 Square Two units as shown on page 25.
5. Repeat steps 1–4 with all the remaining 13½" squares, always combining a light background print square with a medium print square (either blue, gray, or tan). When you have cut and stitched all the 13½" squares, you will have 36

Square Two

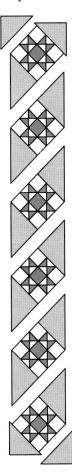

light-and-blue Square Two units, 24 light-and-gray Square Two units, and 12 light-and-tan Square Two Units.

6. Join the Square Two units with the 4" light-medium background print squares and the 4" blue, gray, and tan squares to make 9 blue, 6 gray, and 3 tan Ohio Star blocks as shown.

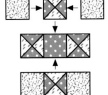

7. Set the blocks together with the light gray setting triangles to make 3 strips as shown. The corner triangles were cut large, to allow some latitude in the finished length of the quilt. Trim the sides of the pieced strips as necessary, leaving a generous ¼" beyond the corners of the star blocks. Trim the tops and bottoms of the strips a generous ¼" or more beyond the corners of the top and bottom blocks.

8. Cut the 8½"-wide "chintz" strips to the same length as the star strips and set the chintz and the star strips together as shown in the photo.

9. Layer with batting and backing; quilt or tie. See page 141 for a quilting suggestion.

10. Bind with straight-grain or bias strips of fabric.

Stars in the Mist, *by Judy Hopkins, 1992, Anchorage, Alaska, 75" x 89". A long-time admirer of chintz strippy quilts, Judy indulged her fondness for neutral colors and minimal contrast by using a collection of soft, muted grays, blue-grays, and tans. Quilted by Beatrice Miller.*

Three and Six ◼◼

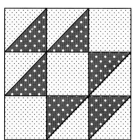

Three and Six
6" block

Dimensions: 68" x 76½"

128 blocks (72 Three and Six and 56 alternate), 6"
set on point 8 across and 9 down; finished without
a border.

Materials: 44"-wide fabric

⅜ yd. each of 9 different light and medium prints
    (ivories, tans, grays, blues, light reds) for bias
    squares and blocks
13" x 13" pieces of 18 different dark prints (reds,
    browns, blues, and blacks) for bias squares
    (Nearest cut is fat quarter.)
2⅝ yds. light background print for alternate
    blocks and setting triangles
4¼ yds. fabric for backing
⅝ yd. fabric for 307" of narrow binding
Batting and thread to finish

Cutting: All measurements include ¼" seams.

From each of the light and medium prints:
    Cut 2 squares, 13" x 13", for a total of 18 large
squares for bias strip piecing.
    Cut 24 squares, 2½" x 2½", for a total of 216
small squares for blocks.

From the light background print:
    Cut 10 strips, 6½" x 42". Cut these strips into a
total of 56 squares, 6½" x 6½", for alternate blocks.
    Cut 2 strips, 9¾" x 42". Cut these strips into a
total of 8 squares, 9¾" x 9¾". Cut twice diagonally
into 32 quarter-square triangles for side setting
triangles. You will have 2 triangles left over.
    Cut 2 squares, 5⅛" x 5⅛". Cut once diagonally
into 4 half-square triangles for the corner setting
triangles.

DIRECTIONS

1. Place one of the 13" light or medium squares
   and one of the 13" dark squares together right
   sides up to cut at the same time. Cut diagonally, corner to corner, to establish the bias,
   then cut bias strips 2⅝" wide. You will have 4
   sets of strips plus 4 corner triangles.

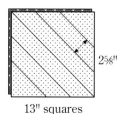

13" squares

2. Stitch bias strips and corner triangles together
   to make 2 pieces of stripped fabric.

3. Cut 24 bias squares, 2½" x 2½", from the
   stripped fabrics, following directions for cutting
   multiple bias squares on page 24.
4. Repeat steps 1–3 with the remaining 13"
   squares, always combining a light or medium
   square with a dark square. You will have a total
   of 432 bias squares.
5. Join the bias squares with the 2½" light or
   medium print squares to make 72 Three and
   Six blocks.

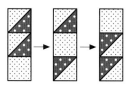

6. Set the blocks together in diagonal rows with
   the light print alternate blocks and side and
   corner triangles. (See "Assembling On-Point
   Quilts" on pages 122–23.) Join the rows as
   shown in the quilt photo. Trim and square up
   the outside edges after the rows are sewn, if
   needed.
7. Layer with batting and backing; quilt or tie. See
   page 141 for a quilting suggestion.
8. Bind with straight-grain or bias strips of fabric.

Three and Six, *maker, date, and place of origin unknown, 64" x 72". The maker's generous and unrestrained use of broad stripes, sometimes cut straight and sometimes off grain, adds zest to this scrappy antique. Note: The pattern uses slightly larger blocks and produces a 68" x 76½" quilt. (Collection of Ella Bosse)*

Tin Man

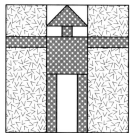

Tin Man
6" block

Dimensions: 40" x 40"

16 blocks, 6", set 4 across and 4 down with 2"-wide sashing; 2"-wide inner border, 3"-wide outer border.

Note: The quilt pictured is made from 9" Tin Man blocks and finishes to 60" x 60". The pattern is written for a more useable, wall-sized quilt.

Materials: 44"-wide fabric

3½" x 13" scraps of 16 different red and rust prints for blocks (Nearest cut is ⅛ yd.)
3" x 13" scraps of 16 different medium and dark blue prints for blocks (Nearest cut is ⅛ yd.)
6½" x 42" strip of light background print for blocks (Nearest cut is ¼ yd.)
⅔ yd. tan or gold print for sashing strips and inner border
½ yd. dark blue print for outer border
1¼ yds. fabric for backing
⅜ yd. fabric for 178" of narow binding
Batting and thread to finish

Cutting: All measurements include ¼" seams.

From each of the red and rust prints:
Cut 1 square, 3¼" x 3¼". Cut twice diagonally into 4 quarter-square triangles. Use 1 of these triangles for the Tin Man's head (A); save 3 for another project.
Cut 1 square, 1" x 1", for neck (B).
Cut 2 rectangles, 1" x 2½", for arms (C).
Cut 1 rectangle, 2¼" x 2½", for body (D).
Cut 2 rectangles, 1" x 3¼", for legs (E).

From each of the medium and dark blue prints:
Cut 2 rectangles, 2" x 2½" (F).
Cut 2 rectangles, 2½" x 4½" (G).

From the light background print:
Cut 1 strip, 1⅞" x 42". Cut this strip into 16 squares, 1⅞" x 1⅞". Cut once diagonally into 32

half-square triangles (H).
Cut 1 strip, 1" x 42". Cut this strip into 1¼"-wide segments, to make 32 rectangles, 1" x 1¼" (I).
Cut 1 strip, 3¼" x 42". Cut this strip into 1½"-wide segments, to make 16 rectangles, 1½" x 3¼" (J).

From the tan or gold print:
Cut 9 strips, 2½" x 42", for sashing and inner border. Cut 2 of the strips into 6½"-wide segments, to make 12 rectangles, 2½" x 6½", for sashing pieces. Leave the remaining strips uncut.

From the dark blue print:
Cut 4 strips, 3½" x 42", for outer border.

DIRECTIONS

1. Piece 16 Tin Man blocks as shown.

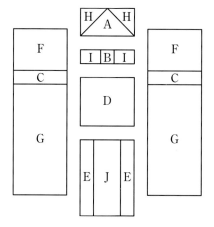

2. Set the blocks together in rows of 4, placing a 2½" x 6½" tan or gold sashing piece between each block as shown.

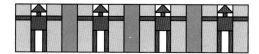

3. Measure the length of the rows and cut 3 of the 2½"-wide tan or gold strips to that measurement for sashing strips. Set the rows together with a sashing strip between each of the rows.
4. Add tan or gold inner border, seaming strips as necessary. See "Borders with Straight-Cut Corners" on page 124.
5. Add dark blue outer border, as for inner border.
6. Layer with batting and backing; quilt or tie. See page 142 for a quilting suggestion.
7. Bind with straight-grain or bias strips of fabric.

Tin Man *by Bridget Hughes Walsh, 1987, Anchorage, Alaska, 60" x 60". Bridget fearlessly combined prints of all descriptions in this charming representational quilt. Her sturdy, red tin men are softened by a smorgasbord of blue background prints. Note: The pattern uses a smaller block to produce a 40" x 40" wall quilt.*

Union

Union
12" block

Alternate block
12" block

Alternate half block
6" x 12" block

Dimensions: 72" x 72"

13 blocks, 12", set as a bar quilt with alternate blocks and half blocks; finished without a border.

Materials: 44"-wide fabric

6 fat quarters of light and dark navy blue patriotic prints

1½ yds. tan background fabric for bias squares

6 fat quarters of tan-background patriotic prints

1½ yds. navy blue star fabric for alternate blocks and half blocks

8 fat quarters of light and dark red fabric for large triangles

½ yd. tan patriotic print for block corners

4½ yds. fabric for backing

⅝ yd. fabric for 292" of narrow binding

Batting and thread to finish

Cutting: All measurements include ¼" seams.

From each fat quarter of navy blue patriotic prints:

Cut 2 squares, 4½" x 4½", for Piece A (See diagram.)

From the tan background fabric for bias squares:

Cut 6 pieces, 13½" x 18". Pair each with a navy blue patriotic print. Cut and piece 6 sets of 2½"-wide bias strips, following the directions for making bias squares on page 23. From this pieced fabric, cut 208 bias squares, 2½" x 2½".

From each of 3 fat quarters of tan-background patriotic prints:

Cut 2 squares, 9" x 9", for alternate blocks.

Cut 1 square, 13¼" x 13¼". Cut twice diagonally into 4 triangles (12 total) for alternate half blocks.

Cut 1 rectangle, 6½" x 12½", for side setting pieces.

From each of the 3 remaining fat quarters of tan patriotic prints:

Cut 2 squares, 9" x 9", for alternate blocks.

Cut 2 rectangles, 6½" x 12½", for side setting pieces.

From the remaining tan background fabric left from bias squares:

Cut 4 squares, 6½" x 6½", for corner setting pieces.

From the navy blue star fabric:

Cut 1 square, 4½" x 4½", for Piece A.

Cut 36 squares, 6⅞" x 6⅞". Cut once diagonally into 72 triangles for alternate blocks and half blocks.

From the red fat quarters:

Cut 4 matching dark red Piece D triangles for each block.

Cut 4 matching light red Piece B triangles for each block.

From the tan patriotic print for block corners:

Cut 52 squares, 2½" x 2½", for Piece C.

DIRECTIONS

1. Piece 13 Union blocks as shown.

Make 13.

2. Piece 12 alternate blocks and 12 alternate half blocks.

3. Join Union blocks with alternate blocks and half blocks into rows, using the photo as a guide. Stitch rows together.

Top bar

Row A

Row B

4. Layer with batting and backing; quilt or tie. See page 142 for a quilting suggestion.
5. Bind with straight-grain or bias strips of fabric.

Union *by Nancy J. Martin, 1992, Woodinville, Washington, 72" x 72". This traditional block, executed in a superb collection of patriotic fabrics, was set together with alternate blocks and half blocks to create a spectacular star setting. Quilted by Nancy Sweeney. (Collection of That Patchwork Place, Inc.)*

Walkabout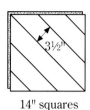

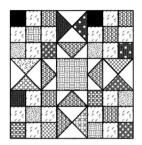

Walkabout
12" block

Dimensions: 61" x 61"

9 blocks, 12", set 3 across and 3 down with 3"-wide pieced sashing strips and sashing squares; 1¼"-wide inner border, 2"-wide pieced middle border, and 6"-wide outer border.

Materials: 44"-wide fabric

10 fat quarters of assorted blue prints
9 fat quarters of assorted pink prints
2 yds. pink print for star tips, pieced sashing, and borders
½ yd. white background fabric for Ninepatch units
⅜ yd. blue fabric for inner border
3½ yds. fabric for backing
½ yd. fabric for 248" of narrow binding
Batting and thread to finish

Cutting: All measurements include ¼" seams.

From each of 9 blue print fat quarters: (Reserve 1 for bias squares in border.)
   Cut 2 strips, 2" x 22", for Ninepatch units.
   Cut 1 square, 3½" x 3½", for star center.
   Cut 1 square, 4¼" x 4¼". Cut twice diagonally into 4 triangles (36 total).
   Cut 1 square, 14" x 14", for Square Two units.

From each pink print fat quarter:
   Cut 1 square, 14" x 14". Pair with 14" blue print squares and cut into 3½"-wide bias strips, following the directions for making bias squares on page 23. From this pieced fabric, cut 60 bias squares, 3⅞" x 3⅞".

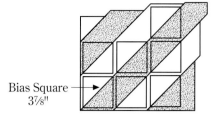

14" squares

Bias Square
3⅞"

To make Square Two units:
   Place 2 bias squares of different coloration with right sides together and seam allowances pressed in opposite directions. Make 60 Square Two units as shown on page 25.

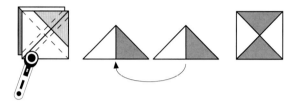

From white background fabric:
   Cut 15 strips, 2" x 22".

From pink print for star tips, sashing, and borders:
   Cut 2 strips 2⅜" x 42". Cut the strips into 34 squares, 2⅜" x 2⅜". Cut 2 additional squares from scraps for a total of 36 squares, 2⅜" x 2⅜". Cut once diagonally into 72 star tips.
   Cut 12 sashing strips, 3½" x 6½".
   Cut 1 piece, 18" x 22", for bias squares in border.
   Cut 6 strips, 6¼" x 42", for outer border.

From the blue fabric for inner border:
   Cut 6 strips, 1¾" x 42".

From the remaining scraps of blue fabric (from fat quarters and inner border):
   Cut 13 squares, 5¼" x 5¼". Cut twice diagonally into 52 triangles for border.
   Cut 22 squares, 3¼" x 3¼". Cut twice diagonally into 88 triangles for border.
   Cut 4 squares, 3½" x 3½", for sashing squares.

Walkabout *by Nancy J. Martin, 1992, Woodinville, Washington, 61" x 61". This quilt was named for fabrics collected during a quilt-teaching trip to Australia. It includes various botanical prints, some by Tony Wentzel, featuring vegetation that one might see on a walkabout. Square Two units surround the star centers and form a secondary star pattern in the pieced sashing. An Aboriginal-type print is used for the Ninepatch units. A printed handkerchief used for the label on the quilt backing is helpful in identifying the Australian flowers found on the fabric. Quilted by Sue von Jentzen. (Collection of That Patchwork Place, Inc.)*

DIRECTIONS

Note: The Walkabout block is made up of Ninepatch and Square Two units. Additional Square Two units are used in the pieced border.

Make 36.   Make 60.

1. Join 2 of the 2" x 22" blue print strips and 1 of the 2" x 22" white background strips; make 7 strip units as shown. The units should measure 5" wide when sewn. Cut the units into 72 segments, each 2" wide.

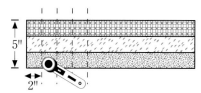

2. Join a 2" x 22" blue print strip and 2 of the 2" x 22" white background strips; make 4 strips as shown. The units should measure 5" wide when sewn. Cut the units into 36 segments, each 2" wide.

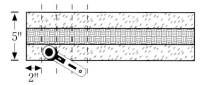

3. Join segments to make 36 Ninepatch units.

Make 36.

4. Combine Ninepatch units, Square Two units, and additional cut pieces to make 9 Walkabout blocks.

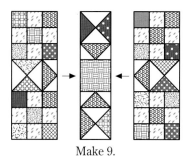

Make 9.

5. Join a Square Two unit to each end of a sashing strip.

6. Join 3 Walkabout blocks and 2 sashing strips to form a row. Make 3 of these rows.
7. Join 3 sashing strips and 2 sashing squares together to form a row. Make 2 of these rows.
8. Join rows together, alternating rows of blocks and sashing squares to form quilt top.
9. Add blue inner border, seaming strips as necessary. See "Borders with Straight-Cut Corners" on page 124. The top should now measure 44½" x 44½". To accommodate the pieced border, adjust width of strips, if necessary, before proceeding.
10. Using the remaining blue print fat quarter and the pink fat quarter, cut and piece 2¼"-wide bias strips, following the directions for making bias squares on page 23. Cut 40 bias squares, 1⅞" x 1⅞", for pieced border.
11. Add pieced border to top as shown, using bias squares and large and small border triangles.

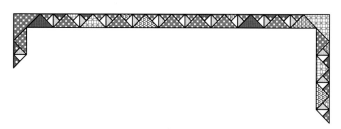

12. Add pink outer border, as for inner border.
13. Layer with batting and backing; quilt or tie. See page 142 for a quilting suggestion.
14. Bind with straight-grain or bias strips of fabric.

Finishing Your Quilt

This section begins with basic information on squaring up blocks and joining them in either straight or on-point (diagonal) sets, and continues with an in-depth discussion of other finishing techniques: adding borders; marking the quilting lines; preparing backing and batting; layering the quilt; quilting and tying; binding; and adding sleeves and labels. A variety of finishing approaches has been used in the quilts included in this book; the photos are an excellent source of ideas.

Common Quilt Terms

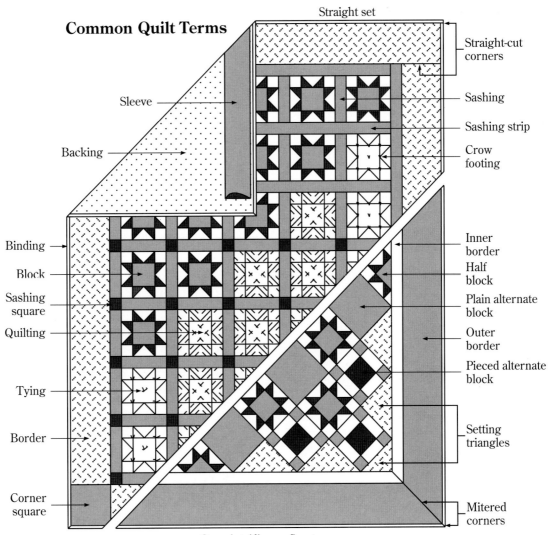

Straight set

Straight-cut corners

Sashing

Sashing strip

Crow footing

Sleeve

Backing

Inner border

Half block

Plain alternate block

Outer border

Pieced alternate block

Binding

Block

Sashing square

Quilting

Setting triangles

Tying

Border

Corner square

Mitered corners

On-point (diagonal) set

Squaring Up Blocks

Some quiltmakers find it necessary to trim or square up their blocks before they assemble them into a quilt top. If you trim, be sure to leave ¼"-wide seam allowances beyond any points or other important block details that fall at the outside edges of the block.

If your block is distorted and doesn't look square, square it up. To do so, cut a piece of plastic-coated freezer paper to the proper size (finished block size plus seam allowance); iron the freezer paper to your ironing board cover, plastic side down. Align the block edges with the edges of the freezer-paper guide and pin. Gently steam press. Allow the blocks to cool before you unpin and remove them.

Straight Sets

In straight sets, blocks are laid out in rows that are parallel to the edges of the quilt. Constructing a straight-set quilt is simple and straightforward. When you set blocks side by side without sashing, simply stitch them together in rows. Then, join the rows to complete the patterned section of the quilt. If you are using alternate blocks, cut or piece them to the same size as the primary blocks (including seam allowances), then lay out the primary and alternate blocks in checkerboard fashion and stitch them together in rows.

When setting blocks together with plain sashing, cut the vertical sashing pieces to the same length as the blocks (including seam allowances) and to whatever width you have determined is appropriate. Join the sashing pieces and the blocks to form rows, starting and ending each row with a block. Then, join the rows with long strips of the sashing fabric, cut to the same width as the shorter sashing pieces. Make sure the corners of the blocks are aligned when you stitch the rows together. Add the side sashing strips last.

If your sashing includes corner squares of a color different from the rest of the sashing (sashing squares), cut the vertical sashing pieces and join them to the blocks to form rows, starting and ending each row with a sashing piece. Cut the horizontal sashing pieces to the same size as the vertical pieces. Cut sashing squares to the same dimensions as the width of the sashing pieces and join them to the horizontal sashing pieces to make sashing strips. Start and end each row with a

sashing square. Join the rows of blocks with these pieced sashing strips.

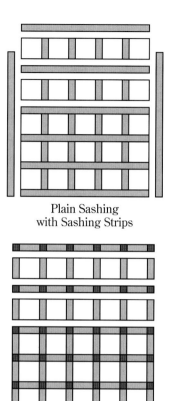

Plain Sashing
with Sashing Strips

Sashing with
Sashing Squares

On-Point Sets

Quilts that are set on point are constructed in diagonal rows, with half blocks and quarter blocks or setting triangles added to complete the corners and sides of the quilt. If you are designing your own quilt and have no photo or assembly diagram for reference, sketch the quilt on a piece of graph paper so you can see how the rows will go together and how many setting pieces you will need.

Plain setting triangles can be quick-cut from squares. You will always need four corner triangles. To maintain straight grain on the outside edges of the quilt, use half-square triangles. Two squares cut to the proper dimensions and divided once on the diagonal will yield the four half-square triangles needed for the corners.

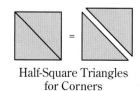

Half-Square Triangles
for Corners

Check your quilt sketch to see how many side triangles are needed. To maintain straight grain on the outside edges, use quarter-square triangles. A square cut to the proper dimensions and divided twice on the diagonal will yield four quarter-square triangles, so divide the total number of triangles needed by four, round up to the next whole number, and cut and divide that many squares. In some cases, you will have extra triangles to set aside for another project.

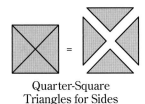

Quarter-Square
Triangles for Sides

How do you determine the "proper dimensions" for cutting these squares? The calculations are based on the finished size of the blocks, and they vary, depending on whether the blocks are set side by side or separated by sashing. Though you can use common mathematical formulas (included below) to calculate the cutting dimensions down to a gnat's eyebrow, I prefer the "cut 'em big and trim 'em down" method, which requires mostly simple addition and just one tedious calculation.

The tedious calculation is this: Multiply the finished size of your block by 1.414 to find the *finished diagonal measurement* of the block. You will need this measurement during the planning stage in order to determine the overall size of the patterned section of an on-point quilt and, later, to calculate the cutting dimensions for setting triangles. If the prospect of translating the result of this calculation from decimals to inches is unnerving, just multiply the finished size of your block by 1.5 to get the *approximate finished diagonal measurement* of the block. The result will be accurate enough for the "cut 'em big" approach to setting triangles.

For on-point sets where the blocks are set side by side with no sashing, determine the proper dimensions to cut the squares as follows:

Corners: Add 2½" to the finished measurement of the block. Cut two squares to that size; cut the squares once on the diagonal.

Sides: Calculate the approximate finished diagonal measurement of the block (finished block size x 1.5); add 3" to the result. Cut squares to that size; cut the squares twice on the diagonal. Each square yields four triangles.

For on-point sets where the blocks are separated by sashing, determine the proper dimensions to cut the squares as follows:

Corners: Multiply the finished width of the sashing by 2; add the result to the finished size of the block, then add 2½". Cut two squares to that size; cut the squares once on the diagonal.
Sides: Add the finished width of the sashing to the finished size of the block. Calculate the approximate finished diagonal measurement (block + sash x 1.5); add 3". Cut squares to that size; cut the squares twice on the diagonal. Each square yields four triangles.

These somewhat slapdash calculations will work just fine; exact numbers are unnecessary. If you ever need to know how to calculate cutting dimensions for setting triangles with utter precision, here are the gnat's eyebrow formulas I mentioned above. First, some basic geometry:

When you know the length of the side of a square or right triangle, multiply by 1.414 to get the diagonal measurement.

When you know the length of the diagonal of a square or right triangle, divide by 1.414 to get the side measurement.

For on-point sets where the blocks are set side by side, with no sashing, determine the proper dimensions to cut the squares as follows:

Corners: Divide the finished block size by 1.414. Add .875 (for seams). Round the result up to the nearest ⅛". (Decimal-to-inch conversions are given on page 122.) Cut two squares to that size; cut the squares once on the diagonal.
Sides: Multiply the finished block size by 1.414. Add 1.25 (for seams). Round the result up to the nearest ⅛". Cut squares to that size; cut the squares twice on the diagonal. Each square yields four triangles.

For on-point sets where the blocks are separated by sashing, determine the proper dimensions to cut the squares as follows:

Corners: Multiply the finished width of the sashing by 2. Add the finished block size. Divide the result by 1.414, add .875 (for seams), and round up to the nearest ⅛". (Decimal-to-inch conversions are given below.) Cut two squares to that size; cut the squares once on the diagonal.
Sides: Add the finished width of the sashing to the finished size of the block. Multiply the result by 1.414, add 1.25 (for seams), and round up to the nearest ⅛". Cut squares to that size; cut the squares twice on the diagonal. Each square yields four triangles.

Decimal-to-Inch Conversions

.125	=	⅛"	.625	=	⅝"
.25	=	¼"	.75	=	¾"
.375	=	⅜"	.875	=	⅞"
.50	=	½"			

ASSEMBLING ON-POINT QUILTS

As mentioned in the previous section, quilts laid out with the blocks set on point are constructed in diagonal rows. To avoid confusion, lay out all the blocks and setting pieces in the proper configuration before you start sewing. In an on-point set where blocks are set side by side without sashing, simply pick up and sew one row at a time; then, join the rows.

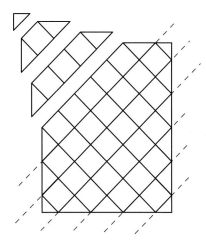

When you use the "cut 'em big" approach for the setting triangles, the side and corner triangles will be larger than the blocks. Align the square corners of the triangle and the block when you

join the side triangles to the blocks, leaving the excess at the "point" end of the setting triangle. Stitch and press the seam, then trim the excess even with the edge of the block. Attach the corner triangles last, centering the triangles on the blocks so that any excess or shortfall is distributed equally on each side.

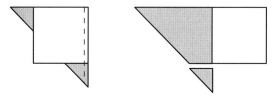

When sewn, your quilt top will look something like this:

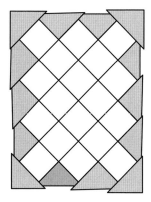

Obviously, you will need to do some trimming and squaring up. At this point, you can make a decision about whether to leave some excess fabric so the blocks will "float" or to trim the setting triangles so that only a ¼"-wide seam allowance remains. Use the outside corners of the blocks to align your cutting guide and trim as desired; make sure the corners are square.

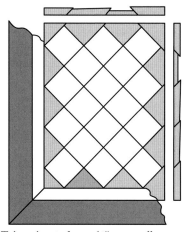

Trimming to leave ¼" seam allowance.
Border, when added, will come to the corners of the blocks.

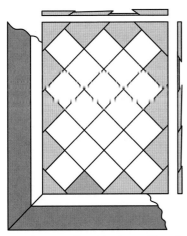

Trim to allow blocks to "float."

The assembly order for on-point sets that includes sashing is a little more complex. You can see from the drawing below that the side setting triangles span a block plus one sashing strip, and the corner triangles span a block plus two sashing pieces. Before laying out your blocks, sashing pieces, and setting triangles in preparation for sewing, make a photocopy or tracing of your paper quilt plan and slice it into diagonal rows so you can see exactly which pieces constitute a particular row. Once you have joined the pieces into rows, start joining the rows from the bottom right corner and work toward the center. When you reach the center, set that piece aside and go to the top left corner, again working toward the center. Add the top right and bottom left corner triangles last, after the two main sections have been joined.

Add corners last.

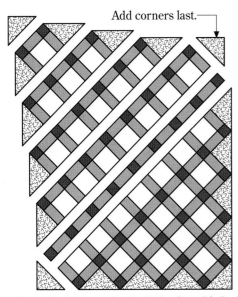

Assembly Diagram for On-Point Set with Sashing

Some of us have difficulty getting on-point quilts to lie flat. You can minimize potential problems by taking a few precautions during the cutting and assembly process. Make sure that the individual blocks are absolutely square and are all the same size. Plain or pieced alternate blocks should be perfectly square and exactly the same size as the primary blocks. The 90° corners of the side setting triangles should be truly square. Since these triangles are quick-cut on the bias, sometimes the corners are not square; it's worth taking the time to double-check. When you join blocks to setting triangles, feed them into the sewing machine with the block, which has a straight-grain edge, on top and the bias-edged setting triangle on the bottom.

BAR QUILTS

In a bar quilt, various pieced and plain units are joined into rows, or bars, instead of blocks; the pattern emerges only after the bars are stitched together. Several different bar formats may be combined to form the overall pattern of a particular quilt. Make sure the design, fabrics, and colors will come out as you intended by laying out the pieces for several bars—or for the entire quilt—before you start to sew.

For some quilts, like the one shown on page 123, bar construction is the only logical method. For many common quilt designs, changing to a bar-quilt approach simplifies construction, reduces the number of seams, and/or creates large seam-free areas in which to quilt. Study a full-quilt photo or a scale drawing of several rows of a quilt to see if old block boundaries can be eliminated and new units of construction identified, as in the examples below.

Traditional Ocean Waves
Blocks in a Diagonal Set

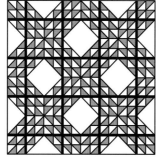

Bar setting simplifies
construction.

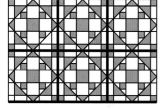

Traditional
Old-Favorite Blocks

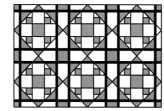

Bar setting reduces
number of seams.

Traditional Hovering
Hawks Blocks

Bar setting creates large
seam-free areas for quilting.

Borders

Whether or not to add a border to your quilt is entirely up to you. Some quilts seem to resist borders. If you have tried several different border options and none seems to work, perhaps the piece wants to be finished without a border at all or with a border on only one or two sides. Many quilts will happily accept a "1-2-3" border—an inner border, a middle border, and an outer border in 1:2:3 proportions (1" inner, 2" middle, and 3" outer borders, or 1½" inner, 3" middle, and 4½" outer borders, for example).

Though many of us avoid adding elaborately pieced borders to our quilts because of the additional work involved, some quilts demand them. As an alternative, try a multi-fabric border. Use a different fabric on each edge of the quilt; use one fabric for the top and right edges and a different fabric for the bottom and left edges; or, join random chunks of several different fabrics until you have pieces long enough to form borders. Quiltmakers who buy fabric in small cuts often resort to multi-fabric borders out of necessity, as they rarely have enough of any one fabric to border an entire quilt!

Because you need extra yardage to cut borders on the lengthwise grain, plain border strips commonly are cut along the crosswise grain and seamed when extra length is needed. Press these seams open for minimum visibility. To ensure a flat, square quilt, cut border strips extra long and trim the strips to the proper length after you know the actual dimensions of the patterned center section of the quilt.

Most of the quilts in the pattern section of this book have seamed borders with straight-cut corners; a few may have borders with corner squares or with mitered corners.

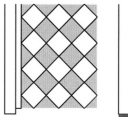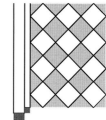

Straight-Cut Corners   Corner Squares   Mitered Corners

Borders with Straight-Cut Corners

To make a border with straight-cut corners, measure the length of the patterned section of the quilt at the center, from raw edge to raw edge. Cut two border strips to that measurement and join them to the sides of the quilt with a ¼"-wide seam, matching the ends and centers and easing the edges to fit. Then, measure the width of the quilt at the center from edge to edge, including the border pieces that you just added. Cut two border strips to that measurement and join them to the top and bottom of the quilt, matching ends and centers and easing as necessary.

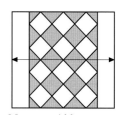

Measure length   Measure width at center
at center.   after adding side borders.

Note: *Do not measure the outer edges of the quilt!* Often, these edges measure longer than the quilt center due to stretching during construction; the edges might even be two different lengths. To keep the finished quilt as straight and square as possible, you must measure the centers.

Borders with Corner Squares

To make a border with corner squares, measure the length and the width of the patterned section of the quilt at the center, from raw edge to raw edge. Cut two border strips to the lengthwise measurement and join to the sides of the quilt with a ¼"-wide seam, matching the ends and centers and easing the edges to fit. Then cut two border strips to the original crosswise measurement, join corner squares to the ends of the strips, and stitch these units to the top and bottom of the quilt, matching ends, seams, and centers and easing as necessary.

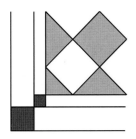

Borders with Mitered Corners

To make mitered corners, first estimate the finished outside dimensions of your quilt *including borders.* Cut border strips to this length plus at least ½" for seam allowances; it's safer to add 2"–3" to give yourself some leeway. If your quilt is to have multiple borders, sew the individual strips together and treat the resulting unit as a single piece for mitering.

Mark the centers of the quilt edges and the centers of the border strips. Stitch the borders to the quilt with a ¼"-wide seam, matching the centers; the border strip should extend the same distance at each end of the quilt. Start and stop your stitching ¼" from the corners of the quilt; press the seams toward the borders.

Lay the first corner to be mitered on the ironing board, pinning as necessary to keep the quilt from pulling and the corner from slipping. Fold one of the border units under at a 45° angle. Work with the fold until seams or stripes meet properly; pin at the fold, then check to see that the outside corner is square and that there is no extra

fullness at the edges. When everything is straight and square, press the fold.

Starting at the outside edge of the quilt, center a piece of 1" masking tape over the mitered fold; remove pins as you apply the tape.

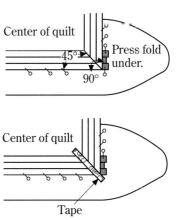

Unpin the quilt from the ironing board and turn it over. Draw a light pencil line on the crease created when you pressed the fold. Fold the center section of the quilt diagonally from the corner, right sides together, and align the long edges of the border strips. Stitch on the pencil line, then remove the tape; trim the excess fabric and press the seam open. Repeat these steps for the remaining three corners.

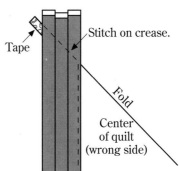

MARKING THE QUILTING LINES

Marking may not be necessary if you are planning to quilt "in the ditch" or to outline a quilt a uniform distance from seam lines. Some quiltmakers do outline quilting "by eye," though many others use ¼"-wide masking tape to mark these lines as they stitch. You can use masking or drafting tape to mark any straight-line quilting design; cut simple shapes from Con-Tact® paper. Apply the tape or adhesive-paper shape when you are ready to quilt and remove promptly after you have quilted along its edge; adhesives left on the quilt too long may leave a residue that is difficult to remove.

Mark more complex quilting designs on the quilt top *before* layering the quilt with batting and backing. A gridded transparent ruler is useful for measuring and marking straight lines and filler grids. You can place quilting patterns from books or magazines or hand-drawn designs underneath the quilt and trace onto the fabric if the quilt fabrics are fairly light. Use a light box or put your work against a window if you have difficulty seeing the design.

If you cannot see through the quilt fabric, you will have to draw the design directly onto the quilt top. Use a precut plastic stencil, or make your own by drawing or tracing the quilting design on clear plastic; cut out the lines with a double-bladed craft knife, leaving "bridges" every inch or two so the stencil will hold its shape. You can also trace the design onto plain paper (or make a photocopy); cover the paper with one or two layers of clear Con-Tact paper and cut out the lines. Try putting small pieces of double-stick tape on the back of the stencil to keep it in place as you mark the quilting lines.

When marking quilting lines, work on a hard, smooth surface. Use a hard lead pencil (number 3 or 4) on light fabrics; for dark fabrics, try a fine-line chalk marker or a silver, nonphoto blue or white pencil. Ideally, marking lines will remain visible for the duration of the quilting process and will be easy to remove when the quilting is done. Light lines are always easier to remove than heavy ones; test to make sure that the markings will wash out after the quilting is completed.

If you are using an allover quilting pattern that does not relate directly to the seams or to a design element of the quilt, you may find it easier to mark the quilting lines on the backing fabric and quilt from the back rather than the front of the quilt.

BACKINGS

The quilt backing should be at least 4" wider and 4" longer than the quilt top. A length of 44"-wide fabric is adequate to back a quilt that is no wider than 40". For a larger quilt, buy extra-wide cotton or sew two or more pieces of fabric together. Use a single fabric, seamed as necessary, to make a backing of adequate size, or piece a simple multi-fabric back that complements the front of the quilt. Early quiltmakers often made pieced backings as a matter of necessity; modern quiltmakers see quilt backings as another place to experiment with color and design.

If you opt for a seamed or pieced backing, trim off selvages before you stitch and press seams open.

Calculate the yardage required for single-fabric backings as follows:
For quilts up to 40" long: width + 6"
For quilts up to 40" wide and longer than 40": length + 6"
For quilts 40–82" wide and up to 82" long: width + 6" x 2 (crosswise seam)
For quilts 40–82" wide and longer than 82": length + 6" x 2 (lengthwise seam.)
For quilts more than 82" wide and up to 126" long: width + 6" x 3 (two crosswise seams.)

BATTING

Batting comes packaged in standard bed sizes; you can also buy it by the yard. Several weights or thicknesses are available. Thick battings are fine for tied quilts and comforters; choose a thinner batting if you intend to quilt by hand or machine.

Thin batting is available in 100% cotton, 100% polyester, and an 80%/20% cotton/polyester blend. The cotton/polyester blend supposedly combines the best features of the two fibers. All-cotton batting is soft and drapable but requires close quilting and produces quilts that are rather flat. Though many quilters like the antique look, some find cotton batting difficult to "needle." Glazed or bonded polyester batting is sturdy and easy to handle, and it washes well. It requires less quilting than cotton and has more loft. However, polyester fibers sometimes migrate through fabric, creating tiny white "beards" on the surface of a quilt. The dark gray and black polyester battings now available may ease this problem for quiltmakers who like to work with dark fabrics; bearding, if it occurs, will be less noticeable.

Unroll your batting and let it relax overnight before you layer your quilt. Some battings may need to be prewashed, while others should definitely *not* be prewashed; be sure to check the manufacturer's instructions.

LAYERING THE QUILT

Once you have marked your quilt top, pieced and pressed your backing, and let your batting "relax," you are ready to layer the quilt. Spread the backing, wrong side up, on a flat, clean surface; anchor it with pins or masking tape. Spread the batting over the backing, smoothing out any wrinkles; then, center the quilt top on the backing, right side up. Be careful not to stretch or distort any of the layers as you work. Starting in the middle, pin-baste the three layers together, gently smoothing any fullness to the sides and corners.

Now, baste the three layers together with a long needle and light colored thread; start in the center and work diagonally to each corner, making a large X. Continue basting, laying in a grid of horizontal and vertical lines 6"–8" apart. Finish by basting around the outside edges.

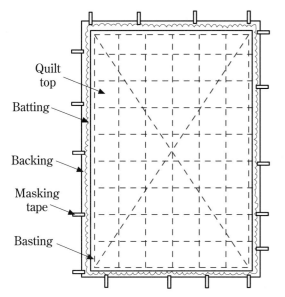

- Quilt top
- Batting
- Backing
- Masking tape
- Basting

QUILTING

The purpose of quilting or tying is to keep the three layers together and to prevent the batting from lumping or shifting. Quilts typically are tied with knots either on the front or the back, or they are machine or hand quilted. Quiet exploration is taking place in this facet of quiltmaking. While several old methods for tying and quilting are being revived, some quiltmakers are stretching tradition by "tying" with eyelets or decorative studs, or quilting with unusual materials, including narrow ribbon, wire, and even cassette tape.

Machine Quilting

Machine quilting is suitable for all types of quilts, from simple baby and bed quilts that will be washed frequently to sophisticated pieces for the wall. With machine quilting, you can quickly complete quilts that might otherwise languish on the shelf. The technique provides some creative challenges as well.

Unless you plan to stitch "in the ditch," mark the quilting lines *before* you layer the quilt. Consider using a simple allover grid or a continuous-line quilting design. Basting for machine quilting is usually done with safety pins; if you have a large work surface to support the quilt and an even-feed foot for your sewing machine, you should have no problem with shifting layers or untidy pleats, tucks, and bubbles on the back side. Remove the safety pins as you sew. Pull thread ends to the back and work them into the quilt for a more professional look.

Try machine quilting with threads of unusual types and weights or experiment with the decorative stitch or twin-needle capabilities of your sewing machine. Double-needle quilting produces an interesting, corded effect.

Traditional Hand Quilting

To quilt by hand, you will need short, sturdy needles (called "Betweens"), quilting thread, and a thimble to fit the middle finger of your sewing hand. Most quilters also use a frame or hoop to support their work. Quilting needles run from size 3 to 12; the higher the number, the smaller the needle. Use the smallest needle you can comfortably handle; the smaller the needle, the smaller your stitches will be.

Thread your needle with a single strand of quilting thread about 18" long; make a small knot and insert the needle in the top layer about 1" from the place where you want to start stitching. Pull the needle out at the point where quilting will begin and gently pull the thread until the knot pops through the fabric and into the batting. Begin your quilting line with a backstitch, inserting the needle straight down through all three layers. Continue by taking small, even running stitches, rocking the needle up and down through all the layers until you have three or four stitches on the needle. Place your other hand underneath the quilt so you can feel the needle point with the tip of your finger when you take a stitch. The hand underneath works in concert with the hand on top to manipulate the needle and fabric to achieve small, even stitches.

To end a line of quilting, make a small knot close to the last stitch; then, backstitch, running the thread a needle's length through the batting. Gently pull the thread until the knot pops into the batting; clip the thread at the quilt's surface. Remove basting stitches as you quilt, leaving only those that go around the outside edges of the quilt.

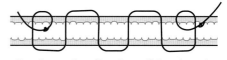

Starting and ending the quilting thread

Utility Quilting

Utility quilting is faster than traditional hand quilting but "homier" than machine quilting; you use big needles and heavy threads (like perle cotton, crochet thread, or several strands of embroidery floss) and take big stitches, anywhere from ⅛" to ¼" in length. The method is well worth considering for casual, scrappy quilts and for pieces you might otherwise plan to machine quilt. Quilts finished with this technique are unquestionably sturdy; the added surface texture is very pleasing.

You can do utility quilting "freehand," without marking the quilt top, or mark quilting lines as usual. Use the shortest, finest, sharp-pointed needle you can get the thread through; try several different kinds to find the needle that works best for you. I like working with #8 perle cotton and a #6 Between needle. Keep your stitches as straight and even as possible.

CROW FOOTING AND OTHER TACKING TECHNIQUES

I have an old comforter in my collection that is tied with a technique called "crow footing." Crow footing is done with a long needle and thick thread, such as a single or double strand of perle cotton or crochet thread. Isolated fly stitches are worked in a grid across the surface of the quilt, leaving a small diagonal stitch on the back of the quilt; there are no visible knots or dangling threads. Stitches can be spaced as far apart as the length of your needle will allow.

Put your work in a hoop or frame. Use a long, sharp-pointed needle—try cotton darners, millinery needles, or soft-sculpture needles. Make a small knot in the thread and insert the needle in the top layer of the quilt about 1" from A. Pull the needle out at A and gently pull the thread until the knot pops through the fabric and into the batting. Hold the thread down with the thumb and insert the needle at B as shown; *go through all three layers* and bring the needle out at C. Insert the needle at D and travel *through the top layer only* to start the next stitch at A.

Work in rows from the top to the bottom or from the right to the left of the quilt, spacing the stitches 2"–3" apart. To end stitching, bring the needle out at C and make a small knot about ⅛" from the surface of the quilt. Make a backstitch at D, running the thread through the batting an inch

or so; pop the knot into the batting and clip the thread at the surface of the quilt.

Crow Footing

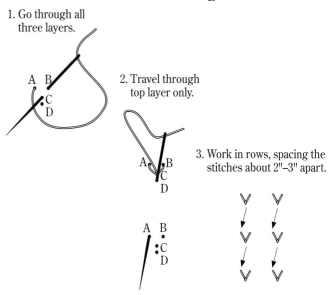

1. Go through all three layers.

2. Travel through top layer only.

3. Work in rows, spacing the stitches about 2"–3" apart.

Other Tacking Techniques

Backstitch tacking is another option. Two favorite stitches are the Mennonite Tack and the Methodist Knot. Both stitches are best worked from the right to the left rather than from the top to the bottom of the quilt; they leave a small horizontal stitch on the back of the quilt.

To do the Mennonite Tack, bring the needle out at A and take a backstitch ¼"–⅜" long *through all three layers,* coming back up just a few threads from the starting point (B-C). Reinsert the needle at D and travel *through the top layer only* to start the next stitch. The tiny second stitch, which should be almost invisible, crosses over the backstitch and locks the tacking.

Mennonite Tack

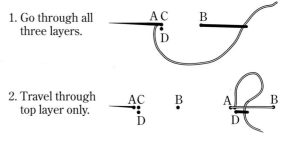

1. Go through all three layers.

2. Travel through top layer only.

3. Work in rows from right to left.

The Methodist Knot is done with two backstitches. Bring the needle out at A and take a backstitch *through all three layers,* coming back up beyond the starting point (B-C). Reinsert the needle at A and travel *through the top layer only* to start the next stitch.

Methodist Knot

1. Go through all three layers.

2. Travel through top layer only to start the next stitch.

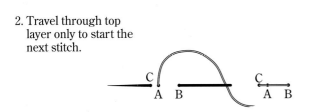

You can lay in any of these tacking stitches at random, rather than on a uniform grid. Early quiltmakers who used these techniques often worked with the quilt stretched full size on a large floor frame, working from both ends and rolling in the edges of the quilt as the rows of tacking were completed, thus eliminating the need for basting. You can tie or tack small quilts without basting if you spread the layers smoothly over a table or other large, flat work surface.

BINDING

When the tying or quilting is complete, prepare for binding by removing any remaining basting threads, except for the stitches around the outside edge of the quilt. Trim the batting and backing even with the edge of the quilt top. Use a rotary cutter and ruler to get accurate, straight edges; make sure the corners are square.

Make enough binding to go around the perimeter of the quilt, plus about 18". The general instructions below are based on ⅜"-wide (finished), double-fold binding, which is made from strips cut 2½" wide and stitched to the outside edges of the quilt with a ⅜"-wide seam. Cutting dimensions and seam widths for bindings in other sizes are given in the chart on page 131.

Straight-grain binding is fine for most applications. Simply cut strips from the lengthwise or crosswise grain of the fabric; one crosswise strip will yield about 40" of binding. For ⅜"-wide (finished) binding, cut the strips 2½" wide. Trim the ends of the strips at a 45° angle and seam the ends to make a long, continuous strip; press seams open.

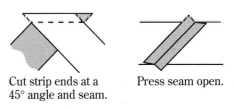

Cut strip ends at a 45° angle and seam.   Press seam open.

Fold the strip in half lengthwise, wrong sides together, and press.

Use bias binding if your quilt edge has curves or if you expect the quilt to get heavy use; binding cut on the bias does wear longer. Some quilters cut bias strips from a flat piece of fabric, joining the strips after cutting; others prefer the tubular method for making a continuous bias strip.

To make flat-cut binding, lay out a length of fabric. (Fabric requirements are given below.) Make a bias cut, starting at one corner of the fabric; use the 45° marking on a long cutting ruler as a guide. Then, cut bias strips, measuring from the edges of the initial bias cut. For ⅜"-wide (finished) binding, cut the strips 2½" wide. Seam the ends to make a long, continuous strip; press seams open. Fold the strip in half lengthwise, wrong sides together, and press.

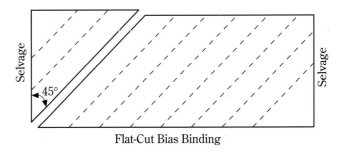

Flat-Cut Bias Binding

For ⅜"-wide (finished) binding made from 2½"-wide bias strips:
¼ yard fabric yields about 115" of binding
⅜ yard fabric yields about 180" of binding
½ yard fabric yields about 255" of binding
⅝ yard fabric yields about 320" of binding
¾ yard fabric yields about 400" of binding
⅞ yard fabric yields about 465" of binding

Continuous bias binding can be made from a square of fabric. To determine what size square will yield the amount of bias binding you need, multiply the length of bias needed (in inches) by the width you plan to cut it, then use a pocket calculator to find the square root of the result.

Let's say you are planning to finish a 72" x 84" quilt with ⅜"-wide finished binding, which requires 2½"-wide strips. You will need 330" of binding (quilt perimeter plus 18"); 330 x 2½ = 825. The square root of 825 is 28.72. Thus, a 29"–30" square will yield the 330" of binding you need.

Remove the selvage and mark the top and bottom of the square with pins. Divide the square on the diagonal to yield two half-square triangles.

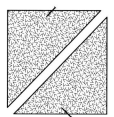

Mark top and bottom of square and divide it on the diagonal.

With right sides together, join the marked sides of the triangles with a ¼" seam; press seam open.

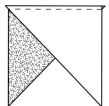

Join the marked sides.

Measure and draw lines the width of the binding strips on the wrong side of the fabric, starting at one of the long, bias edges as shown in the drawing below. If the distance between the last line and the bottom edge is less than the strip width you need, trim to the line above. Slice along the top and bottom lines (at the ends closest to the seam) for a distance of about 6" as shown.

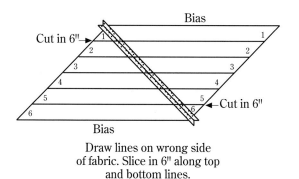

Draw lines on wrong side of fabric. Slice in 6" along top and bottom lines.

With right sides together *and the edges offset by the width of one line,* stitch the ends together to form a cylinder; press seam open. Starting at the top, cut along the marked lines to form a continuous bias strip. Fold the strip in half lengthwise, wrong sides together, and press.

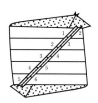

Stitch ends together to form a cylinder, offsetting edges by width of one line.

Cut along lines to form a continuous strip.

Two different methods of applying the binding to the quilt are described below. One produces a binding with mitered corners, with the binding applied in a continuous strip around the edges of the quilt. In the second method, measured lengths of binding are applied separately to each edge of the quilt. In both cases, the instructions given are based on ⅜"-wide finished binding; you will need to use a different seam width if your finished binding is narrower or wider than ⅜".

Bindings with Mitered Corners

For a binding with mitered corners, start near the center of one side of the quilt. Place the binding on the front of the quilt, lining up the raw edges of the binding with the raw edges of the quilt. Using an even-feed foot, sew the binding to the quilt with a ⅜"-wide seam; leave the first few inches of the binding loose so that you can join or overlap the beginning and ending of the binding strip later. Be careful not to stretch the quilt or the binding as you sew. When you reach the corner, stop the stitching ⅜" from the edge of the quilt and backstitch; clip threads.

Turn the quilt to prepare for sewing along the next edge. Fold the binding up and away from the quilt; then, fold it again to bring it along the edge of the quilt. There will be an angled fold at the corner; the straight fold should be even with the top edge of the quilt.

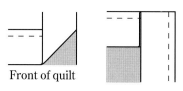

Front of quilt

Stitch from the straight fold in the binding to the next corner, pinning as necessary to keep the binding lined up with the raw edge of the quilt. When you reach the next corner, stop the stitching ⅜" from the edge of the quilt and backstitch; clip threads. Fold the binding as you did at the last corner and continue around the edge of the quilt. When you reach the starting point, fold one end of the binding at a 45° angle; overlap the fold with the other end of the binding and finish stitching.

Fold the binding to the back, over the raw edges of the quilt; the folded edge of the binding should just cover the machine stitching line. Blindstitch the binding in place, making sure your stitches do not go through to the front of the quilt. At the corners, fold the binding to form miters on the front and back of the quilt; stitch down the folds in the miters.

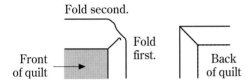

Bindings with Measured Strips

Use this binding method if the outside edges of your quilt need to be eased to the binding so that their finished measurements conform to the quilt's center measurements. Straight-grain binding strips work best for this type of binding.

Bind the long edges of the quilt first. Measure the length of the quilt at the center, raw edge to raw edge.

Note: *Do not measure the outer edges of the quilt.* Often the edges measure longer than the quilt center due to stretching during construction; the edges might even be two different lengths.

From your long strip of binding, cut two pieces of binding to the lengthwise center measurement. Working from the right side of the quilt, pin the binding strips to the long edges of the quilt, matching the ends and centers and easing the edges to fit as necessary. Use an even-feed foot and sew the binding to the quilt with a ⅜"-wide seam. Fold the binding to the back, over the raw edges of the quilt; the folded edge of the binding should just cover the machine-stitching line. Blindstitch the binding in place, making sure your stitches do not go through to the front of the quilt.

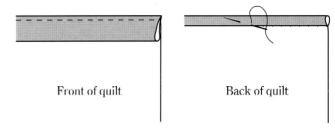

Now prepare and sew the binding strips for the shorter edges of the quilt. Measure the width of the quilt at the center, outside edge to outside edge. From the remainder of your long binding strip, cut two pieces to that measurement plus 1". Pin these measured binding strips to the short edges of the quilt, matching the centers and leaving ½" of the binding extending at each end; ease the edges to fit as necessary. Sew the binding to the quilt with a ⅜"-wide seam.

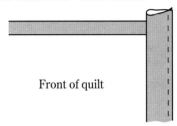

To finish, fold the extended portion of the binding strips down over the bound edges; then, bring the binding to the back and blindstitch in place as before.

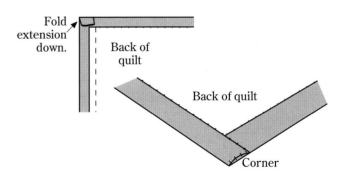

Strip and seam widths for double-fold bindings in various finished sizes are as follows:

Binding	Strip Width	Seam
¼"	1¾"	¼"
⅜"	2½"	⅜"
½"	3¼"	½"
⅝"	4"	⅝"
¾"	4¾"	¾"

SLEEVES AND LABELS

Quilts that will be displayed on walls should have a sleeve tacked to the back near the top edge, to hold a hanging rod. I put sleeves on all my quilts, even those intended for beds, so they can be safely hung if they are suddenly requested for an exhibit or if their owners decide to use them for decoration rather than as bedding.

Sleeves should be a generous width. Use a piece of fabric 6"–8" wide and 1"–2" shorter than the finished width of the quilt at the top edge. Hem the ends. Then, fold the fabric strip in half lengthwise, *wrong* sides together; seam the long, raw edges together with a ¼" seam. Fold the tube so that the seam is centered on one side and press the seam open.

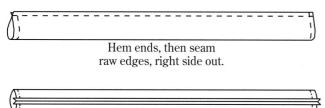

Hem ends, then seam
raw edges, right side out.

Center seam and press open.

Place the tube on the back side of the quilt, just under the top binding, with the seamed side against the quilt. Hand sew the top edge of the sleeve to the quilt, taking care not to catch the front of the quilt as you stitch.

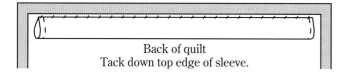

Back of quilt
Tack down top edge of sleeve.

Push the front side of the tube up so the top edge covers about half of the binding (providing a little "give" so the hanging rod does not put strain on the quilt itself) and sew the bottom edge of the sleeve in place as shown at top right.

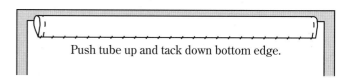

Push tube up and tack down bottom edge.

Slide a curtain rod, a wooden dowel, or a piece of lath through the sleeve. The seamed side of the sleeve will keep the rod from coming into direct contact with the quilt. Suspend the rod on brackets. Or, attach screw eyes or drill holes at each end of the rod and slip the holes or eyes over small nails.

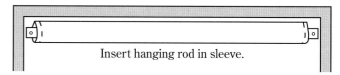

Insert hanging rod in sleeve.

Be sure to sign and date your work! At the very least, embroider your name and the year you completed the quilt on the front or back of the quilt. Quilt historians and the future owners of your quilts will want to know more than just the "who" and "when." Consider tacking a handwritten or typed label to the back of the quilt that includes the name of the quilt, your name, your city and state, the date, whom you made the quilt for and why, and any other interesting or important information about the quilt.

Press a piece of plastic-coated freezer paper to the wrong side of the label fabric to stabilize it while you write or type. For a handwritten label, use a permanent marking pen; use a multistrike ribbon for typewritten labels. Always test to be absolutely sure the ink is permanent!

Note: Hand- or typewritten labels that safely pass the washing-machine test sometimes run and bleed when they are dry-cleaned.

Quilting Suggestions

Each diagram represents a corner of the quilt unless otherwise noted.

Amish Ninepatch Scrap
(without borders)

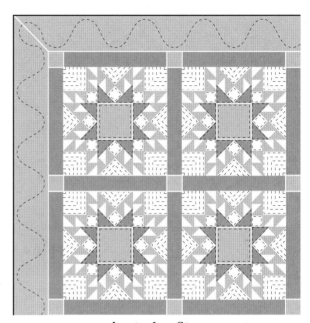

Amsterdam Star

Art Square

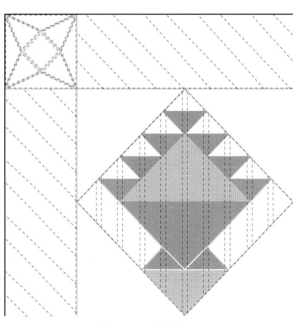

Baskets of Chintz

Bridal Path

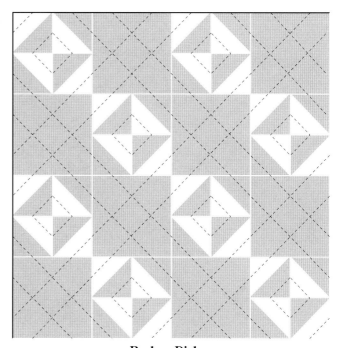

Broken Dishes
(without border)

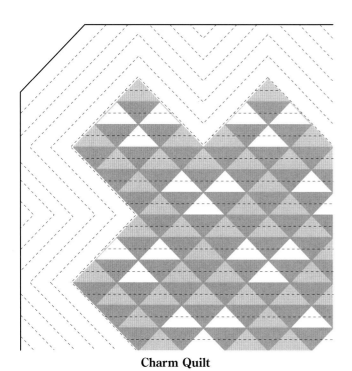

Charm Quilt

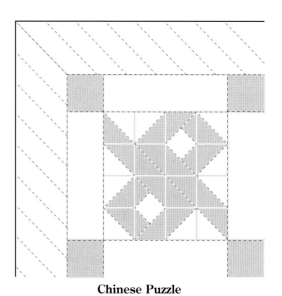

Chinese Puzzle

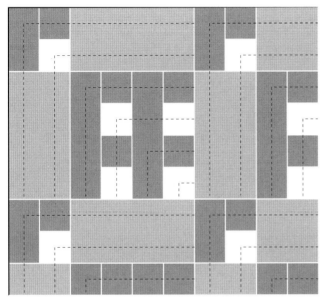

City Lights
(without border)

Cleo's Castles in the Air
(without border)

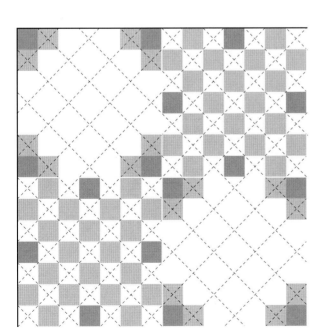

Double Irish Chain
(without border)

Double Wrench

Fine Feathered Star

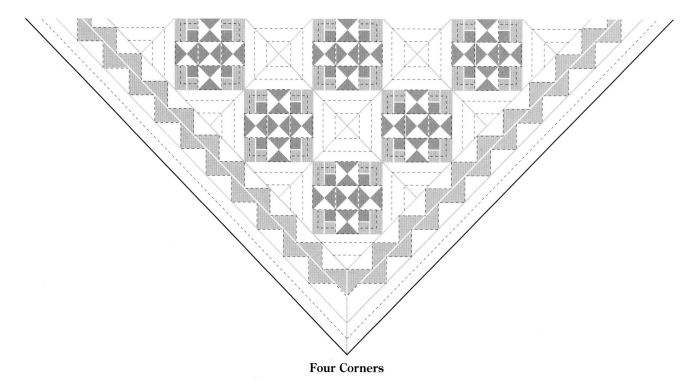

Four Corners

Hearts and Hourglass

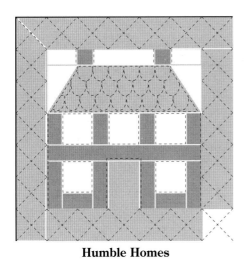

Humble Homes

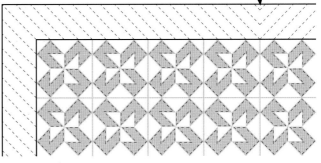

Change quilting direction at midpoint of border.

Jack-in-the-Box

Market Square
(without border)

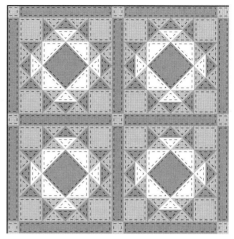

Memory Wreath
(without border)

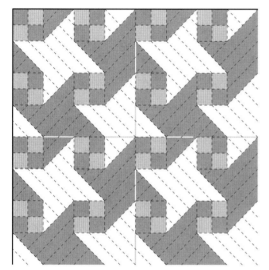

Milky Way

Mrs. Keller's Ninepatch
(without border)

Ocean Chain

Ohio Fence

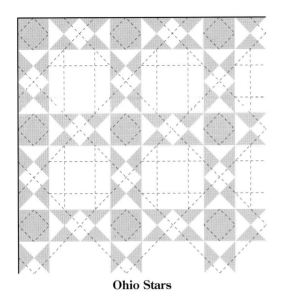

Ohio Stars

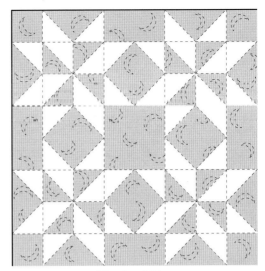

Pinwheel Star
(without border)

Pot of Flowers

Puss in a Corner

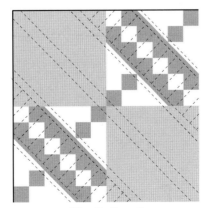

The Railroad

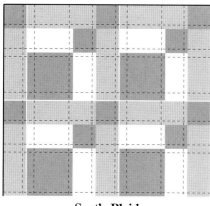

Scot's Plaid

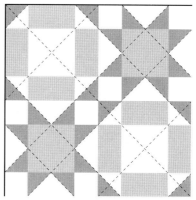

Shoo Fly Star
(without border)

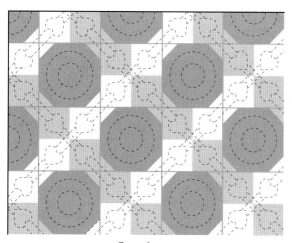

Snowbows
Corner of quilt (shown without borders)

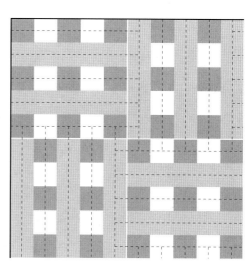

Split Rail Fence
(without border)

Square on Square
(1 block)

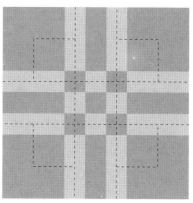

Squares and Strips
(1 block)

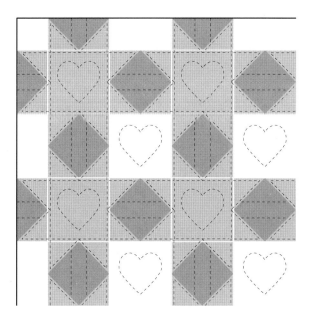

Stars in the Sashing

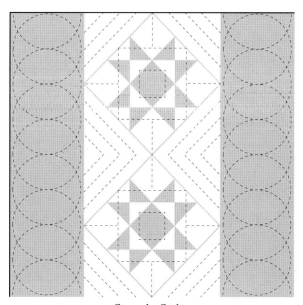

Stars in Strips

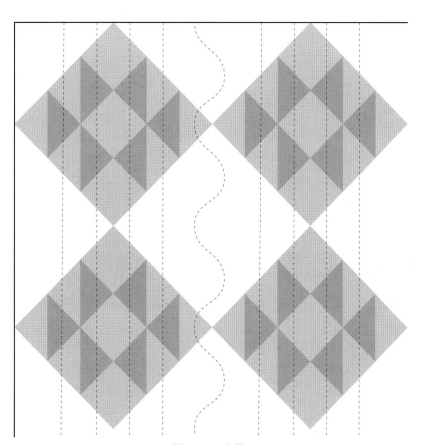

Three and Six

Tin Man
(1 block)

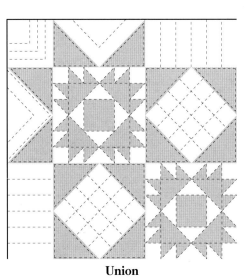

Union

Walkabout